THE GREAT PENDULUM
OF
BECOMING

THE GREAT PENDULUM
OF
BECOMING
Images in Modern Drama

by Nelvin Vos

CHRISTIAN
UNIVERSITY
PRESS

A subsidiary of Christian College Consortium
and Wm. B. Eerdmans Publishing Company
Grand Rapids, Michigan

To
Robert Thornburg and Harold Stenger
who, as friends and true colleagues,
have sustained me within the communitas *of learning*

Copyright © 1980 by Christian College Consortium
1776 Massachusetts Ave., N.W., Washington, D.C., 20036

Order from:
Wm. B. Eerdmans Publishing Company
255 Jefferson Ave., S.E., Grand Rapids, Michigan 49503

Library of Congress Cataloging in Publication Data
Vos, Nelvin.
The great pendulum of becoming.
1. Drama—20th century—History and criticism.
I. Title
PN1861.V67   822'.91'09   80-10772
ISBN 0-8028-1828-5

CONTENTS

ACKNOWLEDGMENTS

This book has grown over the years, and I am grateful to those who have nourished it. To Muhlenberg College and its President, John H. Morey, I owe thanks for granting me a sabbatical leave to begin this study, and through its Faculty Research Committee, for later providing financial resources to complete the manuscript. The staff of the Muhlenberg College Library, particularly the late Mrs. Valborg Jepsen, has also patiently helped me with my research at many points. Particularly, I have appreciated the personal encouragement of Philip Secor while he was Dean of the College.

The notes in the volume attempt to acknowledge the many debts I owe to playwrights, directors, and commentators. Among the many critics whose writings have directed my thinking about drama, I would like to single out Ruby Cohn, Tom F. Driver, John Killinger, and especially William Lynch, S. J., who spent a year on our campus as the Trexler Visiting Professor.

For permission to reprint and revise previously published material, I thank the editors and publishers of *Christian Scholar's Review, Educational Theatre Journal, Muhlenberg Centennial Essays,* and *Salesian Studies.* An earlier version of the chapter on Samuel Beckett was first presented at the annual meeting of the Modern Language Association in December, 1972.

Finally, I am grateful to my present and former students of English 85 (Contemporary Drama), in whose presence I teach, and far more important, I continue to learn.

Muhlenberg College   NELVIN VOS

THE GREAT PENDULUM OF BECOMING:
A Modern World Picture

Hollow men in the wasteland eating their naked lunches while waiting for Godot. A long day's journey into night which ends in the abyss. The Age of Anxiety under the mushroom cloud in the global village. Nausea because there is no exit. At the endgame, the bald soprano chants: "Who's Afraid of Virginia Woolf?"

Such a pointillistic sketch of the modern temper, as we all know, has both truth and distortion about it. To assume that these images constitute the total vision of Western post-World War II literature would be presumptuous. Yet, few would deny the dominant tone of the last half century can be found in the roots of the two words: desperation and despair. The crisis for most modern men is a loss of hope, for the Great Chain of Being, so well described by A. O. Lovejoy,[1] has obviously been broken; the Elizabethan World Picture, evoked by the writing of E. M. W. Tillyard,[2] has faded, if not disappeared. And the breaking and the fading of the old order has left us not with a vacuum, as some have insisted, but with another image. This image, the great Pendulum of Becoming, is still in the process of formation and difficult to discern, for we ourselves are part of it. By using, however, the seminal writings of Lovejoy and Tillyard as foil and counterpoint, we may be able to perceive a dominant model which controls the

[1] Arthur L. Lovejoy, *The Great Chain of Being* (New York: Harper and Row, 1936).

[2] E. M. W. Tillyard, *The Elizabethan World Picture* (New York: Random House, 1944).

1

kaleidoscopic images cited in the opening paragraph and which may provide a metaphor to open up the literature of our time.

— I —

Conceivably, by a drastic flourish of Occam's famous razor, we could reduce the long history of Western literature to four periods: Classical, Medieval, Renaissance, and Modern. What is striking is that the first three periods, amid all their differences, possess an overwhelmingly common characteristic: the presence of order. And the concrete manifestation of describing this phenomenon of order and hierarchical correspondences was found in the image of a chain, or more specifically, the image of a ladder. By now we often feel so threatened by order—or rather by what we feel to be its corollaries, abstraction and interchangeability—that we find it difficult to believe that order was once considered one of the glories of creation. The chain of being and the ladder—now too frequently transformed into the chain of command and the organizational chart—were once matters and metaphors of both comfort and inspiration.

To the earlier literary artist, the idea that reality had several distinct and related classes provided a rich framework for the imagination. The idea of order drew its premise from the belief in a universal, hierarchical order of correspondences that gave a place and purpose to all creation from the greatest to the least, in the heavens, the ranks of society, and the faculties of the mind. In Lovejoy's words, the conception of the universe as a Great Chain of Being was composed

> of an immense, or—by the strict but seldom rigorously applied logic of the principle of continuity—of an infinite, number of links ranging in the hierarchical order from the meagerest kind of existents, which barely escape nonexistence, through every 'possible grade' up to the *ens perfectissimum*—or, in a somewhat more orthodox version, to the highest possible kind of creature, between which and the Absolute Being the disparity was assumed to be infinite—every one of

them differing from that immediately above and that immediately below it by the 'least possible' degree of difference.[3]

One also recalls that Tillyard in *The Elizabethan World Picture* described the Chain of Being as stretching "from the foot of God's throne to the meanest of inanimate objects."[4] At the bottom of the scale was the inanimate class, things, possessing merely existence. The next class, plants, possessing existence and life, was the vegetable class. Animals, the sensitive class, possess existence, life, and feeling. The next class was man, possessing existence, life, feeling, and understanding. The highest class on the ladder, angels, possesses understanding but not the lower faculties.

All of the links below man were considered as subservient to man's purposes; the beings above man, in turn, had the power and the wisdom to influence human actions. The entire model is cosmocentric; indeed, Tillyard insists, "solidly theocentric."[5]

Douglas Bush, another prominent historian of ideas of the Middle Ages and particularly of the Renaissance, argues that "the philosophy of order" was pervasive, and adds that this order was present not only in nature, but also in society:

> The center and foundation was of course Christian faith and theology, with its conception of God and the nature and destiny of man. Then the whole universe, from God down to inanimate nature, is a hierarchy of being. It is the glory, and the peril, of man that he occupies a middle position, linked on the one hand with the angels and God, on the other with the beasts. He is endowed with a rational soul, which should rule over his appetites and passions as God rules over the forces of nature. What holds for the universe and the individual also holds for society, which is not a chaotic aggregate of individuals but a hierarchical organism in which everyone has his place and function. Thus the individual soul and society and the cosmos constitute one inter-related order.[6]

[3]Lovejoy, p. 59.
[4]Tillyard, p. 26.
[5]Tillyard, p. 4.
[6]Douglas Bush, *Classical Influences in Renaissance Literature* (Cambridge: Harvard University Press, 1952), p. 50.

This interrelated order, made metaphorically vivid in the images of the chain and the ladder, manifested itself, according to Lovejoy, in three ordering principles: the principle of gradation, the principle of plenitude, and the principle of continuity.[7]

To ascend a scale to the highest good, whether in Plato's contemplative ideal in the *Symposium* or in Dante's climb to Paradiso, indicates that the approach to perfection must be step-by-step rather than by supernatural flight or direct assault. Even the damned in Dante's *Inferno* have their own inverse hierarchy; Hell itself with its concentric circles as well as Heaven's spheres is part of the divine order. Adam's angelic schoolmaster in *Paradise Lost* instructed his pupil to use each of the scales of nature as a means to what lay above them on the vast slope of being:

> . . . *the scale of Nature set*
> *From center to circumference, whereon*
> *In contemplation of created things*
> *By steps we may ascend to God.* (V, 539–540)

Such gradation is implied in the model of the universe as a ladder of being.

According to Lovejoy, the second principle, that of plenitude, implies "that every link in the Chain of Being exists, not merely and not primarily for the benefit of any other link, but for its own sake, or more precisely, for the sake of the completeness of the series of form. . . ."[8] Fullness, richness, abundance, multiplicity, variety—this cluster of characteristics marked the created order because the Creator Himself is a being of plenitude. Lovejoy points out that Cardinal Bellarmino in his treatise *De ascensione mentis in Deum per scalas creaturarum* elaborates the principle concisely:

> God willed that man should in some measure know him through his creatures, and because no single created thing could fitly represent the infinite perfection of the Creator, he multiplied creatures, and bestowed on each a certain degree of

---

[7]Lovejoy, pp. 24 ff.
[8]Lovejoy, p. 186.

goodness and perfection, that from these we might form some idea of the goodness and perfection of the Creator, who, in one most simple and perfect essence, contains infinite perfections. . . .

Raise now, my soul, the eye of thy mind towards God, in whom are the ideas of all things and from whom, as from an inexhaustible fountain, this well-nigh infinite variety springs. . . .[9]

But this abundance of variations did not lead to fragmentation and chaos, but rather to the final principle of continuity. Coherency and unifying relationships are the earmarks both of a philosophical system such as that of Aquinas and of the catechisms of the Reformation. Harmony reigns; the images of the dance and of the music of the spheres convey the root meaning of belonging to a *uni*-verse. Lovejoy cites a letter of Leibniz which provides a kind of summary of the world view which we have been attempting to draw in outline form:

> All the different classes of beings which taken together make up the universe are, in the ideas of God who knows distinctly their essential gradations, only so many ordinates of a single curve so closely united that it would be impossible to place others between any two of them, since that would imply disorder and imperfection. . . .
>
> And, since the law of continuity requires that when the essential attributes of one being approximate those of another all the properties of the one must likewise gradually approximate those of the other, it is necessary that all the orders of natural beings form but a single chain, in which the various classes, like so many rings, are so closely linked one to another that it is impossible for the senses or the imagination to determine precisely the point at which one ends and the next begins. . . .[10]

All is Being, and Being is One.

Thus, from Aeschylus to the early Ibsen with Shakespeare as a kind of exemplar, one can propose that a common

[9]Quoted in Lovejoy, p. 91.
[10]Quoted in Lovejoy, pp. 144–145.

assumption was the objective existence of an ordered cosmic background. When a man fell, he frequently fell to the lower rung of animality because in his *hubris* he had attempted to assault the angelic realm of perfection. In his famous discourse on the dignity of man, Pico della Mirandola imagines the Creator concluding an address to man with these words: "Thou shalt have power to decline unto the lower or brute creatures. Thou shalt have power to be reborn unto the higher, or divine, according to the sentence of thy intellect."[11] Such a double vision of the realm of the cosmic order supplied the norms for judging an Agamemnon, an Othello, or a Rosmersholm. Shakespeare's plays, prefigured in Greek tragedy and echoed later in the theatre of Schiller and Hugo, stretched the whole of Being on the rack until inevitably the normal order was again restored by the drums of Fortinbras or the calm voices of Kent and Edgar. Such drama is truly cosmic, not only in the sense of encompassing all of reality, but also in the etymology of the term "cosmic," for the drama's setting is harmonious within an orderly universe.

To say that the modern temper does not assume such a world is a truism. A breakout from the accepted cosmic order of the medieval world in a titanic enterprise of establishing a new order by the dominant assertion of man's own power— that is the ultimate pattern of the spiritual revolution beginning in the Renaissance and culminating in this century. And it is a pattern of revolt against what the Middle Ages would have called man's "creaturely" status, the concept of essential dependence implied in the notion of being created. The change of standpoint is ultimately from one which sees man as part of a greater pattern to one which sees him primarily as

[11]Cited in Bush, *The Renaissance and English Humanism* (Toronto: University of Toronto Press, 1939), p. 96. Cf. Bush's *Science and English Poetry* (New York: Oxford University Press), pp. 11, 15, 16. Among other commentators who uphold the thesis of the hierarchy of being as a key to the medieval and Renaissance world view are C. S. Lewis, *The Discarded Image* (Cambridge: Cambridge University Press, 1964), Marjorie Hope Nicolson, *The Breaking of the Circle* (New York: Columbia University Press, 1960), and Leo Spitzer, *Classical and Christian Ideas of World Harmony* (Baltimore: Johns Hopkins Press, 1963).

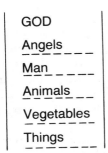

Figure 1: **The Ladder of Being**

pattern's creator. Certainly one of the implications of what the term "modern" implies is the disintegration of the Chain of Being and the collapse of the ladder of hierarchical order.

Therefore, it would be important to explore more precisely what may be a meaningful model which illumines both ourselves and our recent literature. In order to clarify the contrast, the two models might first be presented in diagrammatic form.

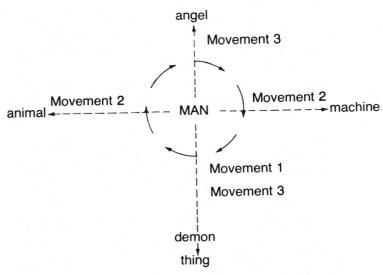

Figure 2: **The Pendulum of Becoming**
(viewed from above)

Figure 2 should be visualized as three-dimensional. The pendulum is suspended above Man and is capable not only of horizontal movement (Movement 2—animal/machine), but also of circular movement (Movement 1—revolving around Man), and of vertical movement (Movement 3—angel/demon/thing). Movement, indeed sometimes erratic movement, marks the model; the more static model of a chain or even a ladder does not appear appropriate for an age which elevates such adjectives as mobile, flexible, open, dynamic, and most of all, free. Modern man thus frequently sees himself as a swinger, existing precariously, but nevertheless hanging on.

It is therefore appropriate that the defining characteristic of a pendulum is its pendency, its state of hanging freely, its ability "to hang loose." To be pending implies that man is in a state, in the root sense of the term, of "during," a condition "while waiting." The restless movement of the pendulum, its indeterminacy, indicates the significance of man not as a being whose nature and substance is set and precise, but as a creature of process, of becoming.

In one of the most important long poems of our time, *Four Quartets*, T. S. Eliot chose as epigraphs two fragments from Heraclitus, the Greek philosopher of flux, both of which illumine the image of the movement of a pendulum:

> Though the law of things is universal in scope, the average man makes up the rules for himself. The way up and the way down are one and the same.

Such thoughts not only echo many of the great modern scientific philosophers such as Darwin, Bergson, and Whitehead, but also reveal themselves in such modern titles as *Right You Are (If You Think So)*, *Remembrance of Things Past*, *As I Lay Dying*, and of course, *Waiting for Godot*.

Thus the oscillation of the pendulum may be understood as the visual image of the dominant presence of relativity in modern man's thinking, whether in physics or in ethics. Even the presumptuousness of describing *the* modern world picture, as Tillyard named his study, must be eschewed, not only because of our proximity to our own age, but also because of the deliberately limited scope which any modern man feels he is able to encompass. Irony is perhaps the literary counterpart of oscillation, for, as Sartre has written, irony "affirms to deny and denies to affirm." Its doubleness catches the nuances of modernity.

Amid the ironies and relativities of modern man, one of the few absolutes of which he feels certain is his own self-consciousness. While the bob of the pendulum may be viewed as the outer self, the mask by which he reveals himself to others, the pendulum itself is suspended from his own self-consciousness. Such an image conveys one of the paradoxical dilemmas of our time: man desires to be a subject only and in control of his own destiny, for this he considers the prerequisite of freedom. He wishes to assert his inde*pendence*. But he also yearns to be seen as object, for only then can he be certain of his existence and particular identity. In dramatic terms, he wishes to be director and producer as well as lead actor, and only if an audience is present can he accept the reality of the performance. Such a position, however, puts a man in a state of de*pendence*, literally, hanging down. As the Manager states in the opening of Pirandello's *Six Characters in Search of An Author*, ". . . you who act your own part become the puppet of yourself. Do you understand?" The leading man's reply suggests the inherent self-destruction in such a position: "I'm hanged if I do." Modern man has become entangled in the strings of his own making; he is imprisoned in the I. Introspection may lead to self-knowledge but also to solipsism as well as paralysis or even madness. We are the children of Freud, and our forebearers are Descartes and Hamlet. Meanwhile, we dangle from our own self-consciousness; we are, as the phrase says, "hung up on ourselves."

— *II* —

The model therefore shows man as central: the scheme is anthropocentric, neither cosmocentric nor theocentric. The major movement (Movement 1) of the Pendulum of Becoming sets the motion for all of the other movements; it revolves around man as he is searching for his self-definition. In such an image, inspiration is understood not as guidance from an external supernatural force, but as an inner source of self-generated creativity. Mimesis of nature and all imitation of divine models is replaced by improvisation and spontaneity from within.

Thus in the image of the ladder, each of the categories is distinct, yet interrelated, while in the pendulum image, each element is arrived at in terms of a metaphor of man: man as machine, man as angel, and so forth. Man does not find his place in relationship to that which is superior or subordinate to him but rather the focus is *multi*faceted, *poly*semous. Instead of the principle of gradation, one finds randomness and aleatoriness, or the counterpart of gradation, monotony, and repetition. Instead of the principle of plenitude, one sees fragmentation and chaos, or the counterpart of plenitude, nothingness, and silence. And instead of the principle of continuity, one senses metamorphosis and explosion, or the counterpart of continuity, incongruity, and absurdity.

Modern art may thus be viewed either as the loss of gradation, plenitude, and continuity, or as the excessive presence of these principles. Much twentieth-century painting and music, as well as the verbal arts, oscillates between these tensions. Paintings by artists as diverse as Jackson Pollack and Piet Mondrian are described as both monotonous and random, cold and silent, explosive and absurd. From Bach to Brahms the end of a musical movement is implied in its beginning, but in a composer such as John Cage, music becomes immediate sense impressions governed mainly by chance. Diffusion, not unity; fragments, not wholes, characterize the artistic achievements in the time of the Pendulum of Becoming. The Chain of Being possesses interpenetration and relationship; it is communal, for all of creation is linked. The Pendulum of Becoming emphasizes discontinuity and caprice; the atmosphere is often one of isolation and alienation. Movement 1 sets the tone for the entire image; if reality is seen primarily as self-reflection, modern man experiences a deep sense of loneliness. He oscillates between an insistence on total independence and a feeling of being victimized, of being held in a permanent state of suspension.

— III —

Movement 2 of the pendulum introduces another dimension not present in the earlier model. Not only is the animal category elevated to an equality with Man, but also the category of machine is added. Inanimate, and yet possessing an independent existence, the image of man as machine is in direct tension with the older tradition of man as animal. And each of the categories both attracts and repels modern man.

Man as animal in its positive aspect emphasizes not only innocence but also harmony with nature. To move towards the animalic is to seek the primitive, the elemental, the preverbal; as Whitman, D. H. Lawrence, and the Romantics would say: "It's warm, even hot, and therefore more lusty, over there." Behavior and instinct, not ethical laws, are the norm; "doing what comes naturally" has had its proponents since Eve. But the line between innocent animality and its negative counterpart, ravenous bestiality, is exceedingly thin, as we shall see as we explore this rich metaphor in the next chapter.

The image of man as machine is more recent. Perhaps finding its theoretical source in deism (the universe as clock), the figure of nature as a machine comes into its own with the "celestial mechanics" of Newton. William Paley in his *Natural Theology* of 1802 likens the universe to a watch and posits a hypothetical but absent God, the Celestial Watchmaker. The image of nature as a machine appears steadily and increasingly throughout the nineteenth century—"the Machine of the Universe—alas!" as Carlyle exclaims in *Heroes and Hero-Worship* in 1841. In the same century, the image of man as a machine surfaces in literary works, particularly as a critique of the effects of the Industrial Revolution. From some of Dickens' novels to Arthur Miller's *Death of a Salesman* and *All My Sons,* the disastrous results of viewing man as machine within a highly organized society have been powerfully portrayed.

In 1914, the critic T. E. Hulme accurately predicted that twentieth-century art was moving toward the creation of forms "associated in our minds with the idea of machinery," toward the time when a sculptor would prefer to organic natural forms "the hard clean surface of a piston rod."[12] Nearly all of Dreiser's novels dramatize the conflict between the individual and the forces of an oppressive industrial society. Steinbeck's Joad family, driven from their land by a tractor owned by big financial interests, become victims of the broken-down automobiles that are the hallmark of their pathetic migration. Ike McCaslin sees his beloved wilderness transformed into a land of hooting locomotives. In all of these, the basic conflict is between man and the machine.

Impersonality, a mere cog in the organization, and eventually the metamorphosis of man into machine marks the bureaucracy of *1984, Brave New World,* and the powerful novels of Kafka, *The Trial* and *The Castle.* Orwell and Huxley, for example, used the myth of Prometheus, inverted. Prometheus brought fire to man, enabling him to become civilized, but was punished by Zeus for treason. Modern man's creations have ended by imprisoning him and placing him on a rock where his liver is eaten by machines. Orwell drew a picture of Big Brother as a kind of Zeus in *1984;* Huxley's *Brave New World* demonstrates a society so organized that it is totally estranged from its human needs; and Kafka's protagonists lose their inner selves when confronted by the impersonal mechanization of society.

Twentieth-century German drama has portrayed many uprisings by workers in plays ranging from Gunter Grass's *The Plebians Rehearse the Uprising* to Brecht's *Saint Joan of the Stockyards* and *The Days of the Commune.* Georg Kaiser's play *Gas II* in 1920 created an overwhelming image of mechanization. As Albert Bermel points out, Kaiser's play is "the mimesis of a

---

[12]"Modern Art and Its Philosophy," in *Speculations: Essays on Humanism and the Philosophy of Art,* ed. Herbert Read (London: Kegan Paul, 1936), pp. 82, 97.

machine."[13] Its language becomes so many cogs and flywheels turning and actuating each other:

> OLD MEN AND WOMEN: *Evening for us!*
> VOICES OF THE OTHERS: *More for us!*
> A VOICE: *What of us?*
> SOME VOICES: *More for us!*
> OTHER VOICES: *What of us?*
> A WAVE OF VOICES: *More for us!*
> A COUNTERWAVE OF VOICES: *What of us?*
> VOICES UPON VOICES: *More for us!*

These are voices without personality, mere machinery in motion. Just as in Ionesco's *The Bald Soprano*, the ending of such a play is not one of denouement, but instead, man as machine disintegrates and self-destructs.

But, just as in the preceding image of man as animal, the image of man as machine possesses within itself positive values such as efficiency, economy, and energetic action. To be mobile can also be viewed as an asset in a time concerned with flexibility. "It's cool, even cold, over there," says the organization man, "but I like the coolness of it all."

Tension also exists between the images of man as animal and of man as machine, for example, in the struggle between aggression (doing what comes naturally) and conformity (doing what others do). Sex as cool, mechanical technique is also in conflict with sex as hot, animalic possession, a microcosmic struggle of the larger oscillation between technology and romanticism in our time, or, in artistic forms, the contrast between cold abstraction, and warm, even hot, naturalism. Man's ambivalence, his swinging between the animalic and the mechanical, reveals itself in our various attitudes and actions towards nature: Shall we subdue and conquer nature— even rape the earth with a device known as the bulldozer and penetrate the sky with a phallic space rocket—or shall we be in harmony with nature, even pantheistically worshipping it? The late Romantics in the guises of the Beat and the Hippie

[13]Albert Bermel, *Contradictory Characters: An Interpretation of Modern Theatre* (New York: E. P. Dutton, 1973), p. 154.

are mutual enemies of the System. Yet, the computer salesman yearns for his weekend hideaway cottage in the
mountains in order to be close to nature, and the young play
their music with the most sophisticated electronic technology
available. And all of us vacillate within the spectrum of alter-
natives.

— *IV* —

In Movement 3 of the Pendulum of Becoming, we swing between the tension of man as angel and man as demon/thing.
To be man as angel is to attempt to be more than human, to
possess the root sin of pride, *hubris*. Yet, at the same time, it is
the way of idealism and perfection. Although the way of
angelic heroism and martyrdom is not as dominant today as in
earlier ages, the pull of the image of man as angel nevertheless
is an inherent element of humanity. Particularly, in the contemporary drama which reconstructs such mythical heroes of
the past as Thomas Becket, St. Joan, and Thomas More, one
finds the oscillation between idealism and self-righteousness.
The link between innocent martyrdom and suicidal self-
destruction is very narrow, especially in a self-conscious age
when such persons probe deeply into their own intentions and
motivations.

The weight however in our time is usually placed in the
other direction, toward man as demon or still further, man as
thing. One aspect of the demonic, for example, can be understood as a synthesis of the negative characteristics of man as
animal and man as machine—the impersonal and mechanical
bestiality of dropping bombs on Hiroshima or lighting ovens
in Belsen and Dachau.

Both categories, man as demon and man as thing, frequently find their source in negation. The power of inversion
and perversion is shown through distortion and deformation of
salient characteristics. While the Greeks fashioned their gods
and goddesses in perfected versions of their own bodies, thus
unifying deity and man, the modern artist, in contrast, has

increasingly regarded the body as a receptacle of depravity and the victim of demonic power. The inadequacy of man is expressed through the ugliness of his flesh. Jack and Robert in Ionesco's early plays and the Killer in his later play are versions of the treacherous reversal of the familiar and hostile. Beckett's visual images of suffering creatures, immobile in garbage cans or with ropes around their necks, stem from aberrations of human relationships and acts. Such impotence, explored more fully in a later chapter, transforms man's humanity into a thing, an inanimate helpless object. On the other hand, Genet, in his nightmare visions of demonic powers, insists that evil is superior to good because it is Nothingness expressed as pure form. The critics Jacobsen and Mueller contrast the biblical emphasis on a creation *ex nihilo* which leads to a plenitude with Genet's reverse process *ad nihilum* which ends in the demonic absence.[14] Infernal and apocalyptic imagery dominate the landscape of much of the modern imagination. Nightmare, not dream, as a later chapter will suggest, describes our fantasy world.

An exhibition in 1969 at the Whitney Museum of American Art entitled "Human Concern/Personal Torment: The Grotesque in American Art" was described by Robert Doty, the Whitney Curator, as "the physical world of man . . . re-examined by artists who view object and environment as malevolent." "For artists of such conviction," wrote Doty, "the world is estranged, life is absurd, the grotesque is the measure of all things, spiritual and material."[15]

The farthest extension of the Pendulum of Becoming thus passes the monstrous and the misshapen and enters the realm of man as inanimate object, or thing. He has lost the energy and movement found in the mechanical images and even the vestiges of humanity still latent in the diabolical forms. He is a blob, a speck, a mere iota in the overwhelming nothingness.

[14]Josephine Jacobsen and William R. Mueller, *Ionesco and Genet: Playwrights of Silence* (New York: Hill and Wang, 1968), pp. 172–173.
[15]Robert Doty, *Human Concern/Personal Torment: The Grotesque in American Art* (New York: Whitney Museum of American Art, 1969), n. pg.

—V—

Antonin Artaud, French theatrical revolutionary in his manifesto of 1938, *The Theater and Its Double,* rejected the history of theatre which limited itself by "its servitude to psychology and 'human interest.' "[16] Such psychological theatre, according to Artaud, reduces the unknown to the ordinary, the mysterious to the banal, causing the theatre's abasement. Artaud's rhetoric certainly exaggerates the inadequacies of the tradition, but his perceptive comments concerning the necessity of the theatre not to forget its primitive rituals, its holy origins, and its metaphysical power provide a prophetic anticipation of much of post-World War II drama.

His proposal for the theatre, in fact, accurately describes the themes and motifs to be explored in this volume's essays: "a theater in which violent physical images crush and hypnotize the sensibility of the spectator seized by the theater as by a whirlwind of higher forces."[17] Later, he explained that such images have their roots in "metaphysical" ideas, ideas which are "all of a cosmic order and furnish a primary notion of a domain from which the theater is now entirely alien."[18] Artaud's specific description of these dramatic ideas, "ideas which touch on Creation, Becoming, and Chaos,"[19] provide the structure for our exploration of the modern theatre.

We begin with the image of Chaos, etymologically, the abyss, the place of yawning. The rubric above the entrance to Dante's Inferno is appropriate: "Abandon all hope, ye that enter here." In the second section, images of Creation, as they are reflected on our modern stages, indicate a quest for Paradise in its attempt to escape homelessness and to recover lost and broken relationships. Finally, in the concluding section, the experience of Purgatorio conjoins several images: process, drama, act. Each of these images connotes movement, a continuous state of Becoming.

[16] Antonin Artaud, *The Theater and Its Double,* trans. Mary Caroline Richards (New York: Grove Press, 1958), p. 90.
[17] *Ibid.,* pp. 82–83.
[18] *Ibid.,* p. 90.
[19] *Ibid.*

In a world longing for meaning, the presence of silence may be an image not only of the void and emptiness of hell or of the meditative awareness of Edenic rest, but also of the pause of expectancy, the time of meanwhile and the interim. A brief exchange from Beckett's *Endgame* may be a microcosm of all three of these possibilities:

> NAGG (clasping his hands, closing his eyes in a gabble):
> *Our Father which art—*
> HAMM: *Silence! In silence!*

"Our Father who art in silence"—this may be the desperate but equivocal prayer of modern man as he is swinging on the Pendulum of Becoming, as he is in the wasteland eating his naked lunch while waiting for Godot, as. . . .

PART I

IMAGES OF CHAOS:
The Confrontation with the Inferno

The heavens themselves, the planets, and this centre
Observe degree, priority, and place,
Insisture, course, proportion, season, form
Office, and custom, in all line of order:
And therefore is the glorious planet Sol
In noble eminence enthroned and sphered
Amidst the other; whose medicinable eye
Corrects the ill aspects of planets evil,
And posts, like the commandment of a king,
Sans check to good and bad. But when the planets
In evil mixture to disorder wander,
What plagues and what portents, what mutiny,
What raging of the sea, shaking of earth,
Commotion in the winds, frights, changes, horrors,
Divert and crack, rend and deracinate
The unity and married calm of states
Quite from their fixture! O, when degree is shaked,
Which is the ladder to all high designs,
The enterprise is sick!
                    —Troilus and Cressida, I, iii, 85–103

ONE

THE BESTIAL:
Metamorphosis into the Animalic

Take but degree away, untune that string,
And, hark, what discord follows! . . .
Then every thing includes itself in power,
Power into will, will into appetite;
And appetite, an universal wolf,
So doubly seconded with will and power,
Must make perforce an universal prey,
And last eat up himself.
                    —*Troilus and Cressida*, I, iii, 109–110, 119–124

Ulysses' speech on degree in Shakespeare's *Troilus and Cres-sida* is undoubtedly literature's most poetic description of the Great Chain of Being, what Ulysses called, "the ladder to high designs." The sun is in command of the planets; the good king who observes "office and custom, in all lines of order," reflects not only the sun but is also the representative of God on earth. If, however, the sun were to lose its imperial place in the heavens, if the king were to abandon, either by default or by the force of others, his high calling, and if God Himself were to be deposed as Lord of the hierarchy of Being, then, "hark, what discord follows!" The effect is anarchy and chaos; the cliché, "all hell breaks loose," takes on new meaning. Instead of the cosmic rule of a just and loving God, order and degree is inverted: "appetite, an universal wolf," is in control. For one of the results of the breakdown of the Chain of Being has been exactly that. Modern drama is pervaded with images of the animalic overwhelming the human, and sometimes in the process, the bestial appetites in self-destruction consume the inner spirit of man.

21

Obviously, to see animalic characteristics in man is not new; writers as diverse as Aristophanes and Molière have satirically observed that man frequently acts like an animal. But the modern imagination has intensified the image of man as animal in several distinct ways. First, instead of the image of man *as* an animal, the modern artist asserts that man *is* an animal; metaphor, not simile, thus becomes the dominant literary figure. In Kafka's strangely powerful and grotesque narrative, *Metamorphosis*, Gregor Samsa has been, in the root sense of metamorphosis, "transferred into" an actual vermin. Second, the image has been universalized. Instead of seeing animal-like characteristics of man, the modern imagination asserts not only that man is an animal, but that all of life itself is bestial. The law of the jungle, only the fit survive—such dogmas from the Darwinian hypothesis have entered the aesthetic climate of our century. Finally, and perhaps most importantly, instead of man's animalistic characteristics being viewed with ridicule and satire and even as a visible sign of infernal powers and man's madness (such as the curse on Nebuchadnezzar), the modern artist frequently portrays the animalic, and even the bestial, as worthy and attractive. The Romantic movement, especially in its intense strand of naturalism, sees man's animal characteristics not only as a revelation of his inner desires but also as a possible redemptive path to maintain or recover his humanity. Modern dramatists are heirs to such reflection, and therefore the Great Pendulum veers sharply toward the animalic in our day.

— *I* —

It will come,
Humanity must perforce prey on itself
Like monsters of the deep.
                                    —*King Lear*, IV, ii, 48–50

To see the animalic images in modern drama in clearest perspective, one could use as counterpoint and contrast no play better than *King Lear*, that great tragedy in which monstrous images, both natural and unnatural, struggle in deep conflict with the human.

The impetus of the tragedy lies in King Lear's blindness to his own folly. By being duped with the flattering phrases of Goneril and Regan and by ignoring the authentic love of Cordelia in the play's opening scene, Lear has rejected the wise and perceptive insight a good king should possess. When faithful Kent attempts to intervene, Lear accurately describes himself: "Peace, Kent!/ Come not between the dragon and his wrath."

The struggle between Lear and his two older daughters now takes on bestial proportions. The king calls Goneril "a detested kite," and laments "how sharper than a serpent's tooth it is/ To have a thankless child!" He warns Goneril that when Regan hears of her cruel actions "with her nails/She'll flay thy wolvish visage." To Regan, he speaks of Goneril's "sharp-toothed unkindness" that is tied, "like a vulture," to his heart, and he adds that Goneril struck him

> with her tongue,
> Most serpent-like, upon the very heart.
> All the stored vengeances of heaven fall
> On her ungrateful top!

But instead of heaven's vengeance falling on the evil daughter ("tigers, not daughters" Albany later calls them), Lear himself is cast out on the heath as a rejected animal:

> I abjure all roofs, and choose
> To wage against the enmity o' the air,
> To be a comrade with the wolf and the owl—
> Necessity's sharp pinch!

Ulysses' account in *Troilus and Cressida* of chaotic inversion recalls not only the fate of Gloucester ("And the rude son should strike his father dead"), but also Lear's inner and outer condition on the hellish heath:

> What plagues and what portents, what mutiny,
> What raging of the sea, shaking of earth,
> Commotion in the winds, frights, changes, horrors,

Divert and crack, rend and deracinate
The unity and married calm of states
Quite from their fixure!
                    —*Troilus and Cressida*, I, iii, 96–101

Throughout the scene on the heath, Edgar as Tom o'Bedlam continues his choric commentary on the inhuman distortions of man turned into beast: "False of heart, light of ear, bloody of hand, hog in sloth, fox in stealth, wolf in greediness, dog in madness, lion in prey." Lear himself in his madness begins to perceive that "Unaccommodated man is no more but such a poor, bare, forked animal," a comment which reflects his earlier lament that "man's life is cheap as beast's."

It is exactly here that Shakespeare's vision stands in direct contrast to the dominant temper in modern drama. Instead of an extended struggle in which each remains animalic to the end of the drama, Lear's descent into the animalic world on the heath is a process of purging and cleansing which leads to his perception of his own full humanity. Verbs of bestial action ("darting," "biting," "gnawing") modulate into the quiet and soft syllables of Lear's confession to Cordelia:

We two alone will sing like birds in the cage.
When thou dost ask me blessing, I'll kneel down
And ask of thee forgiveness. So we'll live,
And pray, and sing, and tell old tales. . . .

The bestial Goneril, Regan, and Edmund have, as Albany predicted, destroyed one another; "humanity must perforce prey on itself/ Like monsters of the deep." By contrast, Lear, in his anguished awareness of his human frailty as he holds the body of Cordelia, has recognized that he is "a very foolish fond old man," weak and feeble, but nonetheless, a man, noble in his suffering. Out of this confrontation with the bestial in nature and within himself, Lear and we with him have perceived once more the rich dimensions of what it means to be fully human.

Modern drama, on the other hand, often invades the bizarre and the grotesque in order to reveal the anguished awareness of our predicament. Such a vision, as we shall see as we recall various plays from the postwar European and American theatre, may awaken us to our deep sense of the loss of the human.

— *II* —

In several of the plays of Eugène Ionesco, the image of the grotesque becomes dramatically vivid in the portrayal of human beings who take on functions and characteristics of animals. Instead of this process leading to self-knowledge, as in Lear, the ending of Ionesco's dramas point to the eventual loss of humanity. In *Jack, or the Submission*, "a naturalistic comedy," as Ionesco called this play, Mother Jack vigorously "paws" and then "sniffs" her prospective daughter-in-law, Roberta. Ionesco indicates in the stage directions at the end of the play that

> the actors utter vague miaows while turning around, bizarre moans, croakings. The darkness increases. We can still see the Jacks and the Robertas as crawling on the stage. We hear their animal noises. . . .

In the sequel to *Jack*, *The Future Is in Eggs*, Roberta and Jack are both purring as the play opens, and later both act as if they were chickens, Roberta by her shrill screeching of "Co-co-codac," and Jack by giving birth to a huge basket of eggs. Such theatre, both in its words and actions, follows Ionesco's dictum that "in the last resort drama is a revelation of monstrosity or some monstrous formless state of being or of monstrous forms that we carry within ourselves."[1]

Rhinoceros does rely heavily on Ionesco's inner mythology, but it also speaks powerfully to the absurd within each of us. To confront the phenomenon that everyone changes into a rhinoceros is indeed absurd, for the action is incongruous, ridiculous, inexplicable. Horrendous and hilarious caprice has taken over; anything may happen in a surreal world. And the

[1]Eugène Ionesco, *Notes and Counter Notes*, trans. Donald Watson (New York: Grove Press, 1964), p. 181.

particular animal Ionesco conjures up in our imagination adds to the grotesque quality of the metamorphosis. Insensitive, thick-skinned, blind, uncontrolled power, "the rhino is," as Ogden Nash has written, "an ugly beast,/ For human eyes, he's not a feast." This pachyderm is a mobile fortress; its trumpetings and howlings indicate a kind of madness at large. In the long soliloquy which concludes the play, Bérenger, the only person not yet turned into a rhino, has not only lost all standards of judgment, but also, more crucially, he has lost his own identity. He is caught in an absurd dilemma: "Now it's too late. Now I'm a monster, just a monster. Now I'll never become a rhinoceros, never, never, never!" The choice for Bérenger is not between animality and his humanity, but between becoming a rhinoceros and seeing himself as a monster, the lone figure who has not experienced a mutation. Both options are images of the grotesque, and Bérenger is left hanging between them. The critic, John Killinger, accurately speaks of the loss of "the stability of humanity" within the play, and adds:

> For Ionesco, there is no anchor, no retaining wall, no boundary to protect something perhaps distinctively human. Being has become fluid and may assume any form or state of consciousness. Nothing guarantees the nature of man.[2]

Indeed, in Ionesco, the very fluidity of being results in anarchy; the impossibility of identifying the human leads to chaos.

— III —

Two plays of the British theatre, John Osborne's *Look Back in Anger* (1956) and Harold Pinter's *The Homecoming* (1965) can be viewed as opposing archetypes of man in relation to animal: the image of escape into innocence and the image of brute power. The two plays both explicitly see their actions on stage

---

[2]John Killinger, *World in Collapse: The Vision of Absurd Drama* (New York: Dell Publishing, 1971), p. 65.

as animalic; in Osborne's play, the place is a "menagerie," "it's more like a zoo every day," and at least four times, someone calls another a "savage." Max, the patriarchal head of the family in Pinter's drama, comments that "they walk in here every time of the day and night like bloody animals." In both plays, a husband passively watches his wife indulge in lovemaking with another man; in *The Homecoming*, Teddy watches his wife copulate with his own brother. The dramatic shock is strong: animals copulate in public, but even animals attack those who interfere with their mating rights.

Amid the similarities between the two plays, the differences are large. In Osborne's play, the animal imagery revolves about squirrels and bears: Alison as a chattering, nervous, skittering figure, and Jimmy, soft and cuddly, but also fierce and cruel. The squirrel bites but the bear overwhelms. As Jimmy describes himself, "the heaviest, strongest creatures in this world seem to be the loneliest. Like the old bear, following his own breath in the forest. There's no warm pack, no herd to comfort him." Alison speaks of their game of bears and squirrels:

> It was the one way of escaping from everything—a sort of unholy priest-hole of being animals to one another. We could become little furry creatures with little furry brains. Full of dumb, uncomplicated affection for each other. Playful, careless creatures in their own cosy zoo for two. A silly symphony for people who couldn't bear the pain of being human beings any longer. And now, even they are dead, poor little silly animals. They were all love, and no brains.

They want, as Jimmy says later, "to escape the pain of being alive." Life as hibernation within these animal roles is the only way they see to regain childhood innocence. Jimmy's words in his concluding speech echo King Lear's phrases to Cordelia quoted earlier, but the total effect is not one of self-recognition, but of retreat from the human:

> We'll be together in our bear's cave, and our squirrel's drey, and we'll live on honey, and nuts—lots and lots of nuts. And we'll sing songs about ourselves—about warm trees and snug caves, and lying in the sun.

The play closes in a lamenting litany: "Poor squirrels" comments Jimmy, to which Alison responds, "Poor bears! Oh, poor, poor bears!" Their withdrawal into the animalic is both anguished and pathetic.

The Homecoming begins in a carnal atmosphere, poised between the chopper and the slab. Max comes through the cave entrance yelling for his scissors; we discover that he was a butcher, and learned to "carve a carcass at his father's knee." He threatens his son Lenny: "I'll chop your spine off talking to your lousy father like that." But Lenny quickly obtains dominance with "Plug it, you stupid sod." Max then attempts to establish power over Sam: ("Isn't it funny you never got married . . . a man with all your gifts"), and then turns on Joey: "You don't know how to defend yourself, and you don't know how to attack."

But Pinter's characters often do know how to defend and how to attack. These "bloody animals" circle, sniff, snarl, and claw at one another. They are nasty and virulent over trifles since the little they have to lose is their all. In this world of the jungle, all trust has been lost, and suspicion therefore breeds menace. Each character is poised for combat, and words are their weapons of power. To Pinter, language is sniper fire: laconic, staccato, precise, designed to cut down the other. Sam, for example, in an effort to regain some status asserts that he has fought in the war, but Max snarls at him, "Who did you kill?" Sam is silent. By the use of quarreling invective, each holds his position as if he were defending a territory.[3]

The males of the play each jockey for a more powerful position over the others. Max begins as top dog, but he is definitely the underdog at the play's conclusion. For it is Ruth who most effectively uses her instincts and cunning, first to destroy Lenny's mask of male bravado, and then later to establish her undisputed right to be the dominant force in the

---

[3]Irving Wardle has perceived the image of the territorial struggle, and views the ethology of Konrad Lorenz, Robert Ardrey, and Desmond Morris as a particularly helpful perspective to understand Pinter's drama. Cf. Irving Wardle, "The Territorial Struggle," in *A Casebook on Harold Pinter's The Homecoming*, ed. John Lahr (New York: Grove Press, 1971), pp. 37–44.

household. By her strategic silences and calculated pauses, by the mere moving of her knee, by her very presence in the room, she has transformed herself, as Wardle comments, into "the queen bee." She has taken possession of the territory, and all of the others have been overwhelmed by her use of sexual dominance. Ruth, in Jessie, Max's wife, has indeed come home; she rules the old cave with icy brute force.

— IV —

American drama has drawn richly from the reservoir of animal imagery, and no play has done so with more amplitude than Eugene O'Neill's *Desire Under the Elms* (1924). This drama sensitively interweaves various images which occur and recur in later postwar American plays.

The image of brute force, the survival of the fit, dominates the play; several characters speak of the deep conflicts as "dog'll eat dog." Basic instincts of possessiveness concerning land, money, and heirs evoke the elemental desires which reside within each of the characters. These elemental desires reveal themselves most strongly in Eben, whose eyes in the opening stage directions of the play are described as "reminding one of a wild animal's in captivity." Animalic fertility and virility shine forth from Eben; Abbie sees him as "a prize bull"; Eben later flaunts the observation that he is "the prize rooster o' this roost." In the time between these two statements, Eben and Abbie have submitted to their lust for one another. When the two lovers first come together, O'Neill remarks that "they stand speechless and breathless, panting like two animals."

The two older brothers, Simeon and Peter, "as naturally unrestrained as beasts of the field," according to O'Neill, "smell of the earth" in their "bovine" crudeness. All of the animals on the farm, Simeon observes, "know them like brothers."

Such an image of the uncivilized primitive and of lusty vitality is combined in Tennessee Williams' creature of "animal joy," Stanley Kowalski, the dominant male in *A Streetcar Named Desire* (1947). Stanley, as he enters bearing the meat home to his wife, heaves the re-stained package to Stella, who laughs breathlessly as she catches it. Stella derisively calls him "pig" and "animal thing," but a few moments later, she and Stanley, according to the playwright, "come together with low, animal moans." Desire again is in control each moment in this play.

Blanche's relationship with Stanley's animal nature is, however, still more ambivalent and complex. She is repulsed by him: "There's something downright—bestial—about him!" But she cannot ignore his astonishing vitality, for he, as Williams described earlier, possesses "the power and pride of a richly feathered male bird among hens." Her long speech to Stella about Stanley is not only a warning to her sister, but also a foreshadowing of Blanche's tragic but inevitable encounter with "the gaudy seed-bearer:"

> He acts like an animal, has an animal's habits! Eats like one, moves like one, talks like one! There's even something—sub-human—something not quite to the stage of humanity yet! Yes, something—ape-like about him, like one of those pictures I've seen in—anthropological studies! Thousands and thousands of years have passed him right by, and there he is—Stanley Kowalski—survivor of the stone age! Bearing the raw meat home from the kill in the jungle! And you—you here—waiting for him!

She concludes her speech with a plea: "Don't—don't hang back with the brutes!" But Blanche's Southern gentility and decorum are only a veneer, and Stanley instinctively senses that amid all their apparent differences, the two share common characteristics of animality. Stanley's designation of Blanche as "Tiger—Tiger" when he confronts her in the powerful rape/seduction scene indicates their common predatory and cunning natures. Both Blanche and Stanley have attempted to gain control of the territory, and particularly of Stella. But in the struggle, Blanche as the "delicate moth" is helpless before the "ape-like" primitive potency of Stanley.

In *The Glass Menagerie* (1944), Amanda, like Blanche, rejects the animal characteristics which her son Tom insists that he owns: "Man is by instinct a lover, a hunter, a fighter. . . ." She berates her son both for eating like an animal and for reading "such filth" as the writing of D. H. Lawrence. Amanda's children follow their animalic temperaments: Tom inherits his wandering instincts, and Laura attempts to escape her painful present by retreating into her glass menagerie. Both offspring therefore reject Amanda, and ironically the cause of the rejection is to be found in her excessive protective mother instinct.

— V —

Several American dramatists have not only portrayed the animal images of brute power, escape, and the primitive, but also have viewed man's identification with animals as a possible way to restore lost relationships with nature and with fellowmen. O'Neill has explored the image of what he has called "belonging to nature" while Edward Albee has dramatized the image of what one of his characters has named, "meeting." And each of these playwrights has written at least one play in which the relationship has been restored, but also written another play in which the attempt to regain the lost relationship was futile, for the animalic appetite conquered the human.

Ephraim, the patriarch of *Desire Under the Elms*, like Lear and like Pinter's Max in *The Homecoming*, feels isolated and therefore lonesome. But unlike Lear, who is forced to live on the heath as an animal by his ungrateful daughters, and unlike Max, who treats his sons and is treated by them as animals, Ephraim by choice forsakes the "lonesome cold" in the house, and goes to the animals in the barn:

> *Down whar it's restful—whar it's warm down t' the barn. I kin talk t' the cows. They know. They know the farm an' me. They'll give me peace.*

Ephraim possesses a sternness as hard as the rocks on his farm, but he at the same time, desires and finds a warmth with nature and animals.

O'Neill constructed one of his plays, *The Hairy Ape* (1922), on the metaphor of man's quest of belonging which ends in the bestial overwhelming the human. One of Yank's fellow workers on a transatlantic liner nostalgically recalls the past in contrast to the present:

> 'Twas them days men belonged to ships, not now. 'Twas them days a ship was part of the sea, and a man was part of a ship, and the sea joined all together and made it one. Is it one wid this you'd be, Yank—black smoke from the funnels smudging the sea, smudging the decks—the bloody engines pounding and throbbing and shaking—wid divil a sight of sun or a breath of clean air—choking our lungs wid coal-dust—breaking our backs and hearts in the hell of the stokehole—feeding the bloody furnace—feeding our lives along wid the coal, I'm thinking—caged in by steel from a sight of the sky like bloody apes in the Zoo!

Yank obviously feels alienated from such a mechanical image of man's selfhood. He therefore rebels against his situation, and attempting to use a lamppost as a club, he attacks people on the street who have called him "a hairy ape." He awakens and thinks he is in the zoo: "Steel. Dis is de Zoo, huh?" But actually, his location is the prison on Blackwell's Island. He escapes from this prison, but in his animalic fury and in his search to find release from his loneliness, he visits the gorilla at the zoo. In the final scene, Yank gradually merges with the ape:

> And why wouldn't yuh get me? Ain't we both members of de same club—de Hairy Apes? . . . It's dis way, what I'm drivin' at. Youse can sit and dope dream in de past, green woods, de jungle, and de rest of it. Den yuh belong and dey don't.

As he opens the cage to shake hands with the ape, the gorilla escapes and closes the door on Yank. As Yank dies, crushed by a murderous embrace from the ape, he asks: "Where do I fit in?" Caught between the mechanical monotony of his imprisoned work which has destroyed his spirit and the lure of the animalic which has now killed his body, Yank belongs to neither. O'Neill accurately commented in the Introduction to the play:

> The subject here is the same ancient one that always was and always will be the one subject for drama, and that is man and

his struggle with his own fate. The struggle used to be with the gods, but is now with himself, his own past, his attempt 'to belong.'

Albee has shifted the focus to man's relationship, not with nature, but with fellow man. George and Martha in *Who's Afraid of Virginia Woolf?* (1962), in order to awaken their deadening and impersonal lives have engaged in "total war." George hears: "Hark! Forest sounds... Animal noises," and that is not unlikely in the violent talk and action taking place in the sedate living room. But within the "total war," Martha confesses about George that it is he "who can hold me, at night, so that it's warm, and whom I will bite so there's blood." The biting and its blood are the price they pay for their warmth. The path to liberation from their illusions and dead routines is to admit that the fears about the big bad wolf are real. To confess such fears is the first step, according to Albee, of being released from the impersonal hell modern man has created for himself.

Two other Albee plays, *The Zoo Story* (1958) and *A Delicate Balance* (1966), each have within them parabolic narratives about animals which are microcosms of the larger human actions. "The Story of Jerry and the Dog," as Jerry calls it, can be juxtaposed with the account of Tobias and the cat.

Jerry himself is a lost animal; seeking, sensitive, belligerent, he possesses the life force and the experience of having faced the worst in man's relationship to man: He's been to the zoo. He knows that in the zoo "everyone is separated from everyone else" just as in his rooming house, he is isolated from others by the beaverboard between each small cubicle of dwelling. The result is loneliness. In desperation Jerry seeks out Peter, and just as in his story he attempts to form a relationship with his landlady's dog. Jerry's description of the spectrum of relationships between the dog and himself reflect the relationship between Peter and himself: indifference, lust, hatred, smiling exploitation, treachery, pity, and most of all, kindness and cruelty. Jerry forces Peter to be aggressive by occupying Peter's favorite territory, the bench, by attacking Peter's masculinity, and by demanding that Peter use his knife. Peter for the first time calls Jerry a "monster," and by assisting Jerry in his death of suicide/martyrdom, he has forsaken his past isolation, his mechanical living, and most of all, his vegetable existence. Jerry's dying comment to Peter, "You're an animal, too," confirms that in their life/death confrontation, each has joined the other in a blood brotherhood.

Tobias in *A Delicate Balance*, on the other hand, does not break through his isolation. The intruding strangers, Harry and Edna, who enter Tobias' life, just as Jerry enters Peter's, carry with them nameless terrors and a hellish vision of the void: "WE WERE FRIGHTENED . . . AND THERE WAS NOTHING." Tobias endeavors to open himself and his home to them, but he is not able to penetrate his own inner shell. So too, he finds it impossible to explain his love and then his hatred of his cat:

> She didn't like me any more. I tried to force myself on her . . . she bit me; hard; and she hissed at me. And so I hit her. With my open hand, I hit her, smack, right across the head. I . . . I hated her! . . . And . . . you see, there was no reason. She and I had lived together and been, well, you know, friends, and . . . there was no reason. And I hated her for that. I hated her, well, I suppose because I was being accused of something, of . . . failing.

He takes her to the vet: "I had her killed." His wife, both rationalizing and yet perceiving the central truth in this relationship, comments: "Well, what else could you have done? There was nothing to be done; there was no . . . meeting between you." Between Tobias and his neighbors and even between Tobias and his wife, there has been no meeting. Instead of Jerry's relationship to the dog, which led to his self-awareness, Tobias can only say about his encounter with others, whether man or animal, "I tried."

—VI—

To encounter the animalic within and around man—this is one of the first experiences Dante portrays as he enters the Inferno in the *Commedia*. Lost in a dark wood, Dante peers into the shadows of what lies ahead. A sense of dream deepening into nightmare pervades the whole opening of the *Commedia*. The sensation is familiar enough—one is caught in a twisted helplessness, with some lovely place of escape just near and open, and the same hindrance, perhaps some horror, interferes. What interferes here is first of all a beast like a leopard, dappled, light, and swift. It does not attack him, but it wanders in front of him, so that he cannot get by. Suddenly he discerns two other creatures—a lion so hungry and fierce that the very air seems shaken with fear, coming terribly against him, and a lean she-wolf. The gaunt wolf so frightens Dante that he turns and runs back

> Like one who loves the gains he has amassed,
>   And meets the hour when he must lose his loot,
>   Distracted in his mind and all aghast,
> Even so was I, faced with that restless brute
>   Which little by little edged and thrust me back,
>   Back to that place wherein the sun is mute.[4]

The animal forces the man back into his tangled and treacherous and dark past, the sun silent and the way wholly lost; only the savage and violent feelings rage chaotically without and within him.

At that very moment, Dante perceives a dim figure, cries to it for help, and it is Virgil who will be Dante's guide and companion through the Inferno. But in modern drama, no such figure, even dimly perceived, appears. Instead, the image left after this kaleidoscopic look at our modern theatre is that the film has stopped precisely at that point where Dante (and we) are thrust back by the fierce and ravenous presence of the beasts. The animalic continues to obstruct the way of the human.

---

[4]Dante, *Hell*, trans. Dorothy L. Sayers (Baltimore: Penguin Books, 1949), I, 55–60.

TWO

IMPOTENCE:
Its Power in Modern Drama

It is a truism to state that nineteenth-century fiction and drama often revolve about the social and moral embarrassment of the presence of an illegitimate child. Not only George Eliot, Charles Dickens, and Thomas Hardy portrayed this situation in important novels of the last century, but Shaw and Ibsen also saw this particular predicament as a dramatic instance of hypocrisy, a living lie which would haunt the wayward all their lives. The flamboyant males who exploited women and who practiced a double standard of morality in such novels and dramas can be juxtaposed with the conniving and scheming women in several of Strindberg's plays.

Amid all the differences in these literary works, the one common thread in such plot situations was the physical act of adultery which led to social and moral destruction. When the moral crisis is one of doubt and faith, the dramatic question becomes: Is he or she faithful? False faith, that is, hypocrisy, must be exposed; honest doubt may lead to social ostracism, but such purging and cleansing may at times restore the fallen to moral perfection once more.

Our century, particularly in its post-World War II decades, finding its dilemmas centered in the crisis of hope and despair, has shifted the focus from illegitimacy to impotence. Instead of casting doubts on the social and moral status of the wayward parent and the unfortunate child, the attention is now on the absence of offspring, the hopeless impossibility of giving birth at all. The bold or brash father and the secretive or manipulative mother have been replaced by the helplessly weak male and the infertile female. Such dramatic situations usually have their source in biological inadequacy, but the relationship frequently implies social and moral impotence as well. In looking more carefully at this image in modern drama, we may see that it reflects one of the most important documents of our time, T. S. Eliot's *The Waste Land,* not only in the barren setting of this poem, but also in the pun of its title which suggests that, for many contemporary men and women, the area near the waist indeed is infertile and impotent.

— I —

In several postwar American plays, such as *Cat on a Hot Tin Roof* and *Who's Afraid of Virginia Woolf?,* the dramatic crisis centers on the inability and the unwillingness to have a child. Biological impotence and sterility may be the initial cause of the problem, but by the end of the plays, it is clear that Brick and Margaret, George and Martha, Nick and Honey, all recognize that the emptiness in their marital lives has its roots in psychological and spiritual weakness. Their evasions of facing the matter directly, without pretense and illusion, are all set within an essentially realistic mode.

The Theatre of the Absurd, however, has contributed an even more overwhelming impression of helplessness in its images of impotence. Both of the tramps in Beckett's *Waiting for Godot* respond eagerly to the expectation that hanging themselves will give them an erection:

> ESTRAGON: *What about hanging ourselves?*
> VLADIMIR: *Hmm. It'd give us an erection.*
> ESTRAGON: *(Highly excited) An erection!*
> VLADIMIR: *With all that follows. Where it falls mandrakes grow. That's why they shriek when you pull them up. Did you not know that?*
> ESTRAGON: *Let's hang ourselves immediately!*

In Arrabal's *Guernica,* the elderly husband responds rhetorically to his wife's taunts: "I can't, can't I? Well, you're the only one who says that. Don't you remember Saturday?" But the old woman's answer, "Which Saturday?" indicates that their relationship has neither a firm physical nor spiritual foundation.

Such fantasy and wishes dominate the actual in many modern plays, especially in the drama of the British playwright, Harold Pinter. Meg, for example, in *The Birthday Party*, her life childless and sterile, treats her strange boarder, Stanley, both as possible lover and potential son. She talks of coming to wake him in his bedroom and of having "some lovely afternoons in that room." But Stanley is so defeated by Lulu calling him a "washout" and especially by Goldberg and McCann's incessant grilling that he becomes a helpless creature, bereft not only of his sanctuary but even of his humanity. In the final brainwashing session, Stanley is speechless, overwhelmed by the staccato assertions of his two accusers:

> GOLDBERG: *Between you and me, Stan, it's about time you had a new pair of glasses.*
>
> McCANN: *You can't see straight.*
>
> GOLDBERG: *It's true, You've been cockeyed for years.*
>
> McCANN: *Now you're even more cockeyed.*
>
> GOLDBERG: *He's right. You've gone from bad to worse.*
>
> McCANN: *Worse than worse.*

The fit survive; obviously, Stanley is not, according to the standard of Goldberg and McCann, socially or morally sound.

Some of the males in Pinter's *Homecoming* are clearly able to bring offspring into the world; both Max and Teddy have three sons. The family's vocation has been that of butchers (they are men of "the chopper and the slab"), but no such bloody aggressiveness appears in the male's subservience to Ruth's domination. Their cigars cannot stay lit; Lenny even confesses, in a typical Pinter conversation ostensibly about the availability of ice for the liquor: "We're got rocks. But they're frozen stiff in the fridge." Divested of virility, unsure of his masculinity, Max does the household chores, cleans, cooks, calls his sons "bitch" and "tit," and speaks with cruel invective—a sadistic joy which gives him a sense of fecundity and power.

At the end of the play, Teddy's response to his wife's decision to abandon him in order to become the wife/lover/

whore of his ancestral home reveals astonishing passivity. Sam also reflects this meekness, for he has continually received abuse from all the others—his one-line revelation about Jessie's immoral past overpowers and kills him. In the last image of the play, Joey is being mothered by Ruth, and Max is pleading to gain attention and love from powerful Ruth: "Kiss me." The "disease" and "plague" which pervades this family is their helplessness, their inability to realize that the presence of love is stronger than any display of power and brute force.

— *II* —

The plays of Eugène Ionesco frequently dramatize characters who are losing or have already lost their power, for objects and impersonal forces have taken over the human. One of his short plays, *The Future Is in Eggs*, finds Jack and Roberta embracing and squatting just as they were at the conclusion of the earlier play, *Jack, or the Submission*. Jack's parents describe the problem:

> FATHER-JACK: *It's three years now since we arranged this marriage. And they've been stuck there ever since caterwauling, with us watching them. And nothing happens.*
>
> MOTHER-JACK: *In spite of all our good wishes and encouragement.*
>
> FATHER-JACK: *Nothing happens, nothing at all! We must get some results quickly.*

The couple is neglecting "the main duty, production," and all of the others encourage them and threaten them to conform to society's requirement of bearing children. Jack suddenly begins to suffer "labor pains," and in agony, groans "Aie! Aie!"—which echoes the "Co-co-codac!" cries of Roberta. Basket after basket of eggs are emptied on "the hatching table," and Jack is required to sit on them. The concluding scene with its proliferation of eggs and the shouts of "Long live production!" combine to create the dramatic situation which appears in many of Ionesco's early plays: impotent human beings are overpowered by the presence of objects and the forces of language.

In the absence of meaning, the words themselves in Ionesco's first play, *The Bald Soprano*, take absolute control, and drive their unfortunate victims wherever their blind energies may chance to direct. Ionesco's own description of the play confirms the barrenness within and without:

> Words had become empty, noisy shells without meaning; the characters as well, of course, had become psychologically empty. Everything appeared to one in an unfamiliar light, people moving in a timeless time, a spaceless space. . . .

The Lesson continues the dominance of language; the professor's bombardment of meaningless words both rapes and kills the student. In *The New Tenant*, a simple poetic image is built up before our eyes, first with a certain amount of surprise, later with relentless inevitability. The helpless protagonist willingly imprisons himself in the midst of endless pieces of furniture.

The barren Old Man and Old Woman in *The Chairs* exist statically in isolation, surrounded by darkness and stagnant water. The proliferation of chairs and the old people's frenetic scurrying around the stage occurs amid the desperate attempt to share their pitiful dreams and remorseful memories. The Old Woman speaks of their son who had "a heart of gold" but abandoned his parents. Denying this, the Old Man reveals their unrealized hopes:

> *Alas, no . . . no, we've never had a child . . . I'd hoped for a son . . . Semiramis, too . . . we did everything. . . .*

Perhaps, as the Old Man had said earlier, "Ah! . . . rived . . . arrived . . . arrived . . . the idiotic bare belly . . . arrived with the rice . . . arrived with the rice . . . ," but "the rice spilled on the ground." Just as the guests are all part of the couple's fantasy, so the son too is a non-existent creature, born of illusion, a product of their infertile and unproductive desires.

Artistic impotence marks Amédée in the drama by that name, for he in the past fifteen years has written only two lines of his play:

OLD WOMAN: *Do you think it will do?*
OLD MAN: *It won't do by itself.*

Meanwhile, the corpse is growing by "geometrical progression," accompanied by the sprouting of poisonous mushrooms all over the flat. Amédée recognizes his own adequacy: "Anyone else could manage better than I do. I'm like a helpless child, I'm defenseless. I'm a misfit."

The three Bérenger plays, *Rhinoceros*, *The Killer*, and *Exit the King*, each portrays the protagonist as a helpless little guy before powers he cannot understand. All have become rhinoceroses; Bérenger absurdly attempts to resist the powers to conform. Facing the Killer, Bérenger questions his own position:

> I don't know anymore, I just don't know. You may be mistaken, perhaps mistakes don't really exist, perhaps it's we who are mistaken to want to exist... say what you believe, can't you? I can't, I can't.

Bérenger stammers his last words: "Oh God! There's nothing we can do. What can we do . . . What can we do. . . ." Just as in *Exit the King*, the power of Death is too overwhelming to resist; Bérenger is impotent before its presence. In each play, Bérenger has no outside resources to call upon. The vacuity of the inner self is apparent; therefore Bérenger, as the other Ionesco protagonists, becomes a passive victim.

— III —

Whether the sense of helplessness before forces one cannot understand is implicitly felt, as in the terror facing the two men in Pinter's *The Dumbwaiter*, or is explicitly articulated as in Stoppard's *Rosencrantz and Guildenstern Are Dead* ("Wheels have been set in motion, and they have their own power, to which we are . . . condemned"), many of the characters in modern drama are paralyzed and immobile in their plight. Their tragic flaw is not that of *hubris*, or of attempting to assault the infinite, or to be as gods, or to be omnipotent. Nor does their fault lie in their attempting to identify either with the efficient energy of a powerful machine or with the aggressive activity of an animal. All of these stances imply a sense of independence and power. Rather, such a victim, in feeling himself surrounded by forces beyond control and at the same time suffering from deep inner *angst,* has abandoned his humanity and succumbed to being part of the world of things, of objects. No more subject of anything, the only relationship is one of object. The bondage is complete; his very dependence has become his tragic flaw. Such a man "hangs down"; he is overwhelmed by a sense of his own contingency. His lack of potency means that he is not involved in his own destiny and if this helplessness is combined with the inability to bring offspring into the world, he possesses no future and no hope. Such a feeling of failure leads to a failure of feeling.

If the drama has its source, as we have seen, in the struggle between power and impotence, then the feeling of love disappears. In the families within the plays of Pinter and Ionesco, the battle for dominance destroys the trust and bonds necessary for loving relationships. Instead of nurturing the bonds which tie men to one another, power is used as a weapon to control the other. The bid for power banishes the human.

"The dread of life," Karl Jaspers has written, "attaches itself to the body." The nameless terrors, the inevitable regrets and the empty memories do not remain only in the mind; they begin to permeate man's whole body until paralysis sets in. Deprived of a strong sense of self, he is fighting to stand still. Complete stasis becomes the only viable position. He does not desire change because, uncertain of who he is, he is even more frightened of what he might become. Since the possibility of becoming, of being transformed, of moving, is the ultimate threat, he by choice and sometimes by default, remains in his present state of helpless chaos and absolute rigidity. In such an ailing world, experience has been quarantined. Such men inhabit that modern space of barren hellishness, the Waste Land.

§ THREE §

THE AMERICAN DREAM TURNED TO NIGHTMARE

In 1654, Captain Edward Johnson announced to the common man weary of the Old World that the land of New England was the place where dreams come true. The title of his book, *A History of New England, or Wonder-Working Providence of Sions Savior,* prepared the reader for his challenging appeal:

> Oh yes! oh yes! oh yes! All you the people of Christ that are here Oppressed, Imprisoned and scurrilously derided, gather yourselves together, your Wives and little ones, and answer to your severall Names as you shall be shipped for His service, in the Westerne World, and more especially for planting the united Colonies of new England. . . . . Know this is the place where the Lord will create a new Heaven, and a new Earth in new Churches, and a new Commonwealth together.[1]

Such a millennial hope inspired Americans in the social, economic, and political spheres for the next three hundred years.

But it was not until 1931 that this force was described specifically as the American Dream. In his history, *The Epic of America,* James Truslow Adams writes that the American Dream is "that dream of a land in which life should be better and richer and fuller for every man, with opportunity for each according to his ability or achievement."[2] Such a vision sees a

---

[1]Captain Edward Johnson, *A History of New England, or Wonder-Working Providence of Sions Savior,* ed. J. Franklin Jameson (New York: Charles Scribner's Sons, 1910, pp. 24–25.
[2]James Truslow Adams, *The Epic of America* (Boston: Little, Brown, and Company, 1931), p. 404.

path leading from log cabin (or haberdashery or drugstore) to the White House, and it honors the ideal of the Alger boy by giving Horatio as a middle name to its offspring. In the sociopolitical world, the dream has been and still is our distinction.

But transformations have taken place within the American Dream in its literary forms. Indeed, in one of Eugene O'Neill's first produced plays, *Bound East for Cardiff* (1916), the main character has a dream of

> *a farm with a house of your own with cows and pigs and chickens, 'way in the middle of the land where yuh'd never smell the sea or see a ship. It must be great to have a wife, and kids to play with at night after supper when your work was done. It must be great to have a home of your own.*

The character's name is Yank.

The particular manifestation of the American Dream as shown in the American theatre reveals itself precisely in the two areas described by Yank. The first is material wealth, whether in land or money, with landed wealth being the ideal. The possession of wealth not only insures economic security, but the owning of land also gives one a sense of identity, of having a meaningful past. But the future is also part of the dream, and here the second concrete fulfillment is shown by the possession of heirs. Children, almost always sons, become a sign that the tangible possessions and the traditions will be handed down to the new generation.

Landed wealth and sons are thus the counters around which much modern American drama has centered its plots and created its characters. In both wishes, the dream of fruitfulness and a bountiful harvest is promised. A scene from Tennessee Williams' play of 1960, *Period of Adjustment*, could be viewed as archetypal. Ralph and Dorothy have "a gorgeously robed statue of the infant Jesus" in their living room. Ralph explains that it is called the Infant of Prague since it was discovered in the ruins of an old monastery of that city, and he adds that it has "miraculous properties: It's s'posed to give you prosperity if you're not prosperous and a child if you're childless."

But the presence, and more often, the distortion and ultimate loss of these two specific hopes has been one of the dominant motifs in more recent twentieth-century American letters. A major strand of American drama is the deliberate inversion of the Puritan ideal as described in the words of Captain Johnson. For the dream is and was essentially a religious ideal. The striving for the concrete goals of landed wealth and heirs becomes that which gives significance and meaning to one's existence, and, if these objectives are not achieved, the result is nightmare, a distortion and inversion of the dream. Paradise is transformed into hell; the disordering of the ideal leads to the fragmentary nightmares, the sudden revelation of hideous truth. Contemporary American theatre is still dramatizing the attempts and the failures to achieve the dream, and thus confronts us with the actualities of deprivation and despair.

— I —

Two playwrights have actually named one of their dramas (*The*) *American Dream*: George O'Neil in 1933 and Edward Albee in 1961. O'Neil's play is the more ambitious of the two; his trilogy, as he calls it, is a panoramic view of American history. Albee's work is a slight one-act play, but its tight construction and skillful characterization overshadow the rather clumsy exposition and melodrama of the earlier play. Yet, and most importantly, both plays find their central plot-conflict in the sons of the family and their claim to the family's name and future. And both plays end in the horror of nightmare.

Since O'Neil's *American Dream* is not well-known, a sketch of its narrative will indicate its metamorphosis from the very beginning of the dream in the seventeenth century to the nightmare of the twentieth century. Act I takes place in 1650 within a colonial household named Pingree, a family which continues throughout the trilogy. The father conceives his life as a response to a God-given challenge: "When England deteriorated in idolatry and vanity, a new land was given miraculously to those who would not yield this consecration to the purity of the word of God spoken through his son." He concludes this speech with a direct appeal to his firstborn, Daniel: "We who are chosen to lead cannot refuse the charge. We are appointed. (He pauses.) You are my eldest son." Although Daniel sees that the land "is the place of fulfillment— an Eden, if you will, waiting for the return of the redeemed exile—the wise Adam," he repudiates his entire legacy by by choosing to marry a barefooted, freedom-living lass from outside the colony instead of the properly prim daughter of the governor. The father has lost his son, and the son has forfeited the property within this "New Canaan," as the father calls it. But Daniel with his love leaves with the dream still in his heart: "This is the land. . . . Now let men stand, each a pillar to the dream that feeds all space. Here—in this land, at last—men shall step into the sun."

Act II finds the family two centuries later in 1849 with another Daniel Pingree as the head of the household. A poor mill hand, he desperately decides to sell the family house, and move to the West: "There's endless promise on the frontier." In his dramatic exit, he accuses the remaining family of following "the Almighty dollar," and he rejects his spiritual inheritance: "If there's a God He's against me, and I'll waste no more time puzzling His will among men. I'll get what I can on this earth."

O'Neil sets the last act of his play in its present time: 1933. The Daniel Pingree of this century is now a worldly success; the setting is a cocktail party celebrating his recent "Guild-of-the-month book." Someone proposes a toast "to this house, which has held what I like to call the American Dream," but an earlier question to Daniel exposes the inner emptiness of the family: "Say, aren't you and Gail ever goin' to propagate?" When Daniel confronts Gail in the process of seducing a guest at the party, Gail flouts the word "Impotent" to him. Daniel confesses his awareness of the void within himself:

> They've all been yapping about America here tonight—this house—the great American epic. Well, I am the American story. . . . Let me spit it out! I'm nothing!

This time, there is no hopeful departure to an open part of New England as in Act I or to the frontier of the West as in Act II. Pingree struggles to a cupboard and kills himself with his pistol. With the last of the Pingrees dies the dream itself.

In Albee's drama of 1961 entitled *The American Dream*, nameless Mommy and Daddy, an affluent urban couple, exchange barren inanities. They have had two sons, and suddenly one appears at the door and announces himself in his own words: "Clean-cut, midwest farm boy type, almost insultingly good-looking in a typically American way. Good profile, straight nose, honest eyes, wonderful smile. . . ." Grandma, resilient with some pioneer determination still present, declares to him:

> Boy, you know what you are, don't you? You're the American Dream, that's what you are. All those other people, they don't know what they're talking about. You. . . you are the American Dream.

But as he speaks, he reveals that inside the handsome shell is only nothingness: "I'll do almost anything for money." He confesses that he is "incomplete" and has experienced "a fall from grace . . . a departure from innocence . . . loss . . . loss." He is incapable of feeling, of being moved, of love and being loved. Separated very early from his identical twin brother whom Mommy and Daddy had destroyed, he has undergone, in Gilbert Debusscher's words, "a progressive mutilation of his spirit and deadening of his flesh."[3] He is now presented to Mommy and Daddy as their newly adopted son, and the audience is left with the image of a marionette farce: the destroyer wife, the emasculated husband, and the corrupt son—indeed, the perfect American family.

But the dramatization of the American Dream and its inversion, the Nightmare, has not been limited to the two plays specifically titled as such. If one looks at the most well-known plays of the major American dramatists of this century—Eugene O'Neill, Arthur Miller, Tennessee Williams,

---

[3]Gilbert Debusscher, *Edward Albee: Tradition and Renewal* (Brussels: American Studies Center, 1967), p. 37.

and Edward Albee—one discovers that the Dream turned to
Nightmare has consistently been a theme of our theatre.[4]
Several versions of the nightmare will be noted, but each is
consistently one of deprivation. Some families have no offspring; others have ne'er-do-wells; and still others lose their
sons, either literally or symbolically, during the dramatic
action. Some families possess neither land nor wealth; others
live in cramped spaces in tight financial straits; and still others
lose their material goods either before or during the action of
the play. Half a dream is not enough; that experience is already a nightmare. Such portrayals of the American family
indeed are a great distance from the views that Captain
Johnson expressed some three hundred years ago. For many of
our most recent writers have made us feel that the world is for
them what Henry James described in his last years—"a nightmare from which there is no waking save by sleep."[5]

—*II*—

Many of the plots from O'Neill's early work in the 1920s to his
unfinished cycle of plays, *A Tale of Possessors Self-Dispossessed*,
published posthumously, find their impetus in the passions for
land and sons. Two of his most highly regarded plays, *Desire
Under the Elms* (1924) and *Long Day's Journey into Night* (written 1941, published 1956), particularly reveal that the society
whose imperfections O'Neill exposed was still wasting itself, as
he once said, in "that everlasting game of trying to possess
your own soul by the possession of something outside it."[6]

[4]Paul N. Siegel, for example, in "The Drama and the Thwarted
American Dream," (*Lock Haven Review*, No. 7 [1965], 52–62) traces the
failure of "the nineteenth-century dream of America as a new society in
which men realize themselves." His insights are particularly perceptive in
revealing this motif in earlier plays such as Barry's *Holiday* and Odets'
Awake and Sing.

[5]Cited in Nathan A. Scott, Jr., *The Broken Center* (New Haven: Yale
University Press, 1966), p. 80.

[6]Cited in John Gassner, *Eugene O'Neill, University of Minnesota Pamphlets on American Writers*, 45 (Minneapolis: University of Minnesota Press,
1965), p. 36.

In *Desire Under the Elms,* the possessiveness of all of the family is dramatized by their constant use of the word "mine." And it is the farm, the land, desired by everyone in the play, which causes the conflicts and intense passions of the play. Each sees the farm as the fulfillment of his dream.

O'Neill names the family the Cabots, that distinguished New England clan which, according to the familiar doggerel, "speaks only to God." The rugged virtues of pioneer idealism and independence are still present in Ephraim Cabot, the family patriarch in the setting of 1850. The dream is still alive in him. But his two older sons are interested in only one subject: "They's gold in the fields o' Californi-a." Simeon and Peter are indeed rock-like, but not in conviction, only in crudeness. The youngest son, on whom the father has placed his future by naming him Eben (Ebenezer—"stone of hope"), has turned into a brooding, morose young man, lamenting his mother's death. Thus Ephraim's name ("the fruitful one") is most ironic, for his three sons are not following in his footsteps.

Ephraim yearns to become fruitful once again, to have Abbie, his new wife, father a son. "A son is me—my blood—mine," as he says simply, "the farm needs a son." A son is indeed born, but as the offspring of Abbie and Eben's lust, the child is doomed. For in the end Abbie and Eben have lost their son and the farm, Ephraim has lost all three of his sons—two to California and the third to prison—and he is to live a bitter, lonely life on the farm. The passionate desires for land and heirs have led only to defeat and destruction.

In *Long Day's Journey into Night,* James Tyrone, a weak patriarchal figure in contrast to Ephraim, desperately attempts to maintain his name and future, but it is a losing cause. His progeny, again all males, are Jamie, age thirty-four, whom his father calls "a damned tramp," and Edmund, whom Jamie rather accurately describes as "only an overgrown kid! Mama's baby and Papa's pet! The family White Hope!" The father has gradually lost touch with his sons as well as his wife through his obsession to speculate in land. He contends that "land is land, and it's safer than the stocks and bonds of Wall Street swindlers." He owns property valued at a quarter of a million dollars, but he insists that he is land poor, and refuses to give his son twenty-five cents for carfare.

Ironically, the Tyrones have never owned a home. During the father's career as a traveling actor in melodramas, the family stayed in second-rate hotels, and now they rent a summer house on the New England coast. And in the course of one long day's journey into one night, James Tyrone has lost all: the sanity of his wife, the respect of his sons, and most of all, his own self-respect. His dreams, like Ephraim Cabot's, have been transformed into nightmare. For both pursued their desire for landed wealth so intensely that they lost their sons who were to inherit it.

In two pivotal plays of Arthur Miller, *All My Sons* (1947), and *Death of a Salesman* (1949), money-seeking fathers are repudiated by their sons, which culminates in the father's self-destruction.

Joe Keller, factory owner, is more interested in personal aggrandizement and society's favor than he is in responsibility for others. The exposé of his personal failure to reject faulty aircraft parts leads to the older son's decision to commit suicide and the younger son's repudiation of his father. Miller portrays Joe Keller not as villainous but as weak. Keller bows to pressure; he is indecisive. When Keller is aware that he is responsible for his own actions, that others, as he says just before the end of the play, are "all my sons," he kills himself. His acquired wealth now is meaningless, for as a neighbor comments earlier: "Money. Money- money- money- money. You say it long enough it doesn't mean anything." In the father's final act of self-destruction, his decisiveness is an attempt to gain his dignity once more. But the dream of a rosy future with wealth and heirs has been shattered.

In Willy Loman, whose vocation is the American archetype of the peddler-salesman, Miller has created a powerful image of the seemingly inherent destruction within the American Dream. The Lomans have two sons, but again they are ne'er-do-wells. Biff is at the unpromising age of thirty-four, unmarried, drifting, with no future in sight, and Happy, the younger son, according to his mother, is "a philandering bum." Both want easy money, and we see in Willy's flashback memory that his failure both to teach and to practice simple honesty has contributed to their waywardness.

Willy and Linda Loman have almost completed the mortgage payments on their home, but Willy complains: "The way they boxed us in here. Bricks and windows, windows and bricks." He has a dream for his family that "before it's all over we're gonna get a little place out in the country, and I'll raise some vegetables, a couple of chickens. . . ." and Biff echoes his father's desire for land; he speaks of buying a ranch "to raise cattle, use our muscles," a place to have freedom and success. But neither the father nor the son accomplishes his goal.

By contrast, Willy's brother, Ben, possesses both sons (all seven of his children are sons) and land, "several properties in Alaska." Ben is crass, ruthless, and extremely proud of his exploits: "Why, boys, when I was seventeen I walked into the jungle, and when I was twenty-one I walked out. *He laughs.* And by God I was rich." He has succeeded; Willy has failed. Still more ideally, Charley, Willy's neighbor, has not only wealth, but also a son, Bernard, who is now a successful lawyer and has two sons of his own.

The Dream therefore is fulfilled for some, but Willy's version of the dream, according to Biff, was "phony." When Willy is convinced that Biff still loves him, he destroys himself to give his sons the $20,000 from his insurance. He dies for his dream: for his sons and money, but Charley perceptively comments at the graveside that Willy "had the wrong dreams. All, all wrong." Biff has gained in self-knowledge by the end of the action, but for Willy, there is little, if any, awareness of his illusions. Just as the opening of the play is described as "a dream arising out of reality," so the drama concludes in a crescendo nightmare of suicide. Ben, Charley, and Bernard are winners; the American Dream has no room for a loser such as Willy.

In contrast, the families in Tennessee Williams' plays once did have landed wealth, but have lost it and are now living in old dreams and fantasies. Williams' first widely known play, *The Glass Menagerie* (1944), initiates the themes of nostalgia and inheritance which are dominant throughout his writing career. Amanda speaks often of her glorious past at

Blue Mountain. But, according to the opening stage directions, the Wingfields are now living in an

> apartment which faces an alley and is entered by a fire-escape,
> a structure whose name is a touch of accidental poetic truth,
> for all of these huge buildings are always burning with the slow
> and implacable fires of human desperation.

In this setting, Tom Wingfield is the male heir, but he rejects
the family's inheritance of self-improvement and stick-to-it-
iveness. Instead of working his way up the ladder of success at
Continental Shoemakers, he curses the job. Tom's dreams are
of adventure and wanderlust, and, at the end, he has repudiated all that his family has stood for. His dreams culmi-
nate only in haunting memories of his past.

Several other plots of Williams' plays are interwoven
with the motif of inheritance. Blanche, the non-heroine of *A
Streetcar Named Desire* (1947), talks longingly of the family's
former Southern estate, Belle Reve. All her meaning in life is
still in that distant past. In *A Period of Adjustment* (1960),
Ralph does have a three-year-old son, but he insists that his
wife has already turned the child into a sissy. Therefore the
father rejects the child and talks of escaping. He wants to buy
a piece of ranchland near San Antone and there herd Texas
Longhorns. The call of the land, past or future, beckons each
of the characters.

No other play Williams has written finds more of its
power in the conflicts of wealth and inheritance than *Cat on a
Hot Tin Roof* (1955). Brick and Margaret are childless in sharp
contrast to his brother Gooper and wife: "Think of it, Brick,
They've got five of them and number six is coming." Margaret
adds that Gooper's wife is "the monster of fertility," and Big
Daddy, patriarchal head of the family who is slowly dying of
cancer, bluntly insists that "Gooper's wife's a good breeder,
you got to admit she's fertile." The inheritance at stake is, as
Big Daddy says, "close to ten million in cash and blue chip
stocks, outside, mind you, of twenty-eight thousand acres of
the richest land this side of the valley Nile!" And Big Mama
very specifically indicates to Brick what is needed to inherit

this "kingdom," a term Big Daddy uses to describe his possessions:

> *Oh, Brick, son of Big Daddy! Big Daddy does so love you! Y'know
> what would be his fondest dream come true? If before he passed on,
> if Big Daddy has to pass on, you give him a child of yours, a
> grandson as much like his son is like Big Daddy!*

Brick's wife schemes, reminiscent of O'Neill's Abbie, to gain
the inheritance and she will most likely succeed. But the
choric refrain of Big Mama is accurate in describing the deep
and violent struggles in this play as well as much of recent
American drama: "Yes, it's just a bad dream, that's all it is, it's
just an awful dream."

With Edward Albee's plays in the late fifties, the focus
has shifted almost entirely to the male heir. Affluence is assumed in each of the families in his plays; his couples are
urbane, sophisticated, and their walls are covered with book-
cases and expensive prints. Yet their lives are empty and hollow. And in the vacuum of boredom, the members of the
families either talk in cliches, or, as George, in *Who's Afraid
of Virginia Woolf?*, says, they dig deep and engage in "Total
War": "When you get down to bone, you haven't got all the
way, yet. There's something inside the bone . . . the marrow . . . and that's what you gotta get at." Only when such
pain is present do Albee's numbed characters seem to be living.

Their deepest anguish is their impotence, spiritual and
psychological, if not biological. In Albee's first play, *The Zoo
Story* (1958), Jerry arouses unimaginative Peter, secure in his
executive position with a small publishing house, with the
following conversation:

> JERRY: *And you have children.*
> PETER: *Yes; two.*
> JERRY: *Boys?*
> PETER: *No, girls . . . both girls.*
> JERRY: *But you wanted boys.*
> PETER: *Well . . . naturally, every man wants a son, but . . .*
> JERRY: *(Lightly mocking) But that's the way the cookie
> crumbles?*

PETER: (Annoyed) *I wasn't going to say that.*
JERRY: *And you're not going to have any more kids,
   are you?*
PETER: (A bit distantly) *No. No more.*

Jerry's most cruel thrust which stimulates Peter to attack is on the same subject.

*Fight for that bench; fight for your parakeets; fight for your cats;
fight for your manhood, you pathetic little vegetable. You couldn't
even get your wife with a male child.*

Peter's flaw appears to be his inability to create a meaningful future. He really had no dreams. He has therefore been condemned to live in a bored and meaningless present until his encounter with Jerry.

The center of Albee's most well-known play, *Who's Afraid of Virginia Woolf?*, is also to be found in that symbol for meaningless existence in our time, impotence. Honey, in her silly drunkenness, may pretend she is a bunny, "Hip, hop. Hip, hop," but, as George says about her miscarriage: ". . . and then the puff went *away* . . . like magic . . . pouf!" Martha may insist that she is the Earth Mother, the ultimate symbol of fecundity, but the major illusion which George and Martha have created together is a hypothetical son, a projection which gives meaning to their lives. In Martha's words, the son is "the one light in all this hopeless . . . darkness . . . our SON." Not until this false security is destroyed— when both George and Martha finally accept that the son is dead—can Martha confess that she now is afraid of Virginia Woolf, that she does possess deep inner fears.

In *A Delicate Balance*, Albee again portrays an elegant couple, Tobias and Agnes, within a wealthy setting. Their thirty-six-year-old daughter has come home, dragging her fourth marriage, as her father says, "like some Raggedy Ann doll, by the feet." More elusive and more threatening to them is the memory of their son, Teddy, who has died long ago. His absence has affected all of their relationships since that time: "It was unreal: I thought Tobias was out of love with me—or, rather, was tired of it, when Teddy died, as if that had been the string." The weakness of Tobias and Agnes' subsequent

taking over to maintain a delicate balance within the family
similar to George's powerlessness and Martha's dominance, all
appear to be rooted, according to Albee, in the ghost-like
presence of the dead male heir who has destroyed the dreams
of the family.

— III —

The Cabots, the Tyrones, the Kellers, the Lomans, the
Wingfields as well as the families of Big Daddy and Big Mama
and Daddy and Mommy have all dreamed the American
Dream, and the dream has changed to Nightmare. *Who's
Afraid of Virginia Woolf?* implies that George and Martha are
all that is left of the first American family.

But what must be insisted upon is that these more recent
negative images find their source and impetus in the dream.
Just as the bleakness of the Inferno can only be realized by
contrast with the riches of Paradise, so the horror of the
nightmare is experienced most vividly by seeing its transfor-
mation from the original dream. More specifically, the presence or absence of landed wealth and heirs is part of the way
in which man conceives his role in the cosmic drama, for such
goals are influenced by his understanding of time and space.

The value of time is certainly one of the main differences
between the people of the dream and the people of the nightmare. In the dream, the past is renounced, the present en-
joyed, and therefore the future is open and pregnant with
possibilities. To possess land and wealth as well as a male heir
is to continue one's name and to be assured of immortality, if
not in heaven, at least in the cherished memory of others. In
the nightmare, one is haunted by the past. This leads to
uncertainty and despair in the present, and therefore the future, if it exists at all, is ominous and foreboding. Time and
history become a burden.

Not only time, but also space is a dimension of the dream
and the nightmare. To be rooted in, and to have one's offspring become heirs to, a particular piece of land is to provide
much more than real estate and security. Such space gives

meaning; it may even, in Mircea Eliade's term, be transformed into a sacred place, an *axis mundi*,[7] that is, the center of the world, the navel of the earth, that out of which one's identity is born. But in the versions of the nightmare we have explored, the meaning of space has been destroyed. All space is the same, which neutralizes the significance of space and erodes the meaningfulness of particular places. Contemporary mobility is not, strictly speaking, a movement to places. Instead, as Tom Driver has pointed out, mobility is "movement to where certain people happen to live, to where they gather, to certain equipment (people plus equipment equal 'the office') or where certain events are scheduled."[8] Such mobility provides the illusion of freedom, but without an *axis mundi*, the feeling is one of alienation and lostness. By contrast, a frontier such as the opening of the West, as R. B. Heilman suggests, "means, space, space implies time, and time a future in which dreams may be realized. On the other hand: no frontier, no space; no space, no time, no future: now or never."[9]

Such a feeling of loss not only affects man's social and economic life, but also his religious understanding. To believe in the promises of a fulfillment of a particular time and place, as the Puritans in New England did, is to have faith and hope for the future. The early Americans, as H. Richard Niebuhr has shown us in his study of *The Kingdom of God in America*,[10] saw their time and place as a fulfillment of those religious promises rooted deep in biblical history. One colonial writer pointed out that Georgia lay "in the same latitude with *Palestine* herself, that promis'd *Canaan*, which was pointed out by

[7]Mircea Eliade, *The Sacred and the Profane,* trans. Willard R. Trask (New York: Harcourt, Brace and Company, 1959), pp. 35–37.

[8]Tom F. Driver, "The Loss of the Histrionic and the Modern Quandary of Theology," *Soundings,* LI (Spring, 1968), 215.

[9]Robert B. Heilman, "The Dream Metaphor: Some Ramifications," in *American Dreams, American Nightmares,* ed. David Madden (Carbondale: Southern University Press, 1970), p. 13.

[10]H. Richard Niebuhr, *The Kingdom of God in America* (New York: Harper and Brothers, 1937).

God's own choice, to bless the Labours of a favorite People."[11]
Another, in a farewell sermon, called Virginia the garden of
the world, "a good land flowing with milk and honey."[12] John
Cotton reminded those who set sail for Massachusetts that
they were the heirs of God's promise to appoint a land of
Canaan for his chosen people: "And therefore the land of
Canaan is called a land of promise."[13]

The American Dream may find its embryonic beginnings
in those two concrete promises given long ago to Father
Abraham. "And I will give you, and to your descendants after
you, the land of your sojournings, all the land of Canaan for
an everlasting possession . . . and moreover I will give you a
son" (Genesis 17:8, 16). Abraham's dream-vision was fulfilled: the land of Canaan flowed with "milk and honey"
(Exodus 33:5), and Isaac was born, whose descendants were to
be "as the stars of heaven and as the sand which is on the
seashore" (Genesis 22:17). Recent American drama has been
centered not in the story of the American Adam, as R. W. B.
Lewis set forth about our nineteenth-century writings,[14] but
rather in the Covenant motif which may well be the framework opening up much of the literature of our time. Our theatre,
even in its seemingly irreligious manifestations, possesses
vestiges of its Judeo-Christian roots and Puritan heritage.

Early Americans dreamed the dream which viewed this
land as the New Canaan. As Eliade points out, the names of
New England, New York, New Haven "express not only the
nostalgia for the native land left behind, but above all the
hope that in these lands and these new cities life will know
new dimensions."[15] But the literary artist of our time has
inverted the vision: the hero is not the innocent Adam, but

[11]Cited in Charles L. Sanford, *The Quest for Paradise* (Urbana: University of Illinois Press, 1961), p. 84.

[12]*Ibid.*

[13]*Ibid.*, p. 176.

[14]R. W. B. Lewis, *The American Adam* (Chicago: University of
Chicago Press, 1955).

[15]Eliade, *The Quest: History and Meaning in Religion* (Chicago, University of Chicago Press, 1969), p. 98.

the fallen Adam who lives east of Eden. The land, although rich in resources, is not Canaan, for it destroys the inner souls of its inhabitants. Sterility and impotence, not fertility, mark the world the American artist portrays. The bonds of love and obedience which the covenant of works with Abraham symbolized have long been lost in our day, but what remains in one aspect of our cultural landscape, the threatre, are the attempts to claim the tangible signs of the promise: land and heirs.

Leslie Fiedler has suggested that "what we dream rather than what we are is our essential truth."[16] By destroying the dream, many of the protagonists in recent American drama destroyed themselves. By cutting off the past, they have discovered that the future is meaningless. By being deprived of heirs and of the land of promise, they must confront the inferno of barrenness and dispossession. And by losing the Dream, they find themselves in the midst of Nightmare.

[16]Leslie Fiedler, *An End to Innocence* (Boston: Beacon Press, 1955), p. 172.

PART II

IMAGES OF CREATION:
The Quest for Paradise

I saw the best minds of my generation destroyed by
    madness, starving hysterical naked,
dragging themselves through the negro streets at dawn
    looking for an angry fix,
angelheaded hipsters burning for the ancient heavenly
    connection to the starry dynamo in the machinery
    of night . . .

—from Allen Ginsberg's *Howl*

§ FOUR §

RECOVERING THE CONNECTION

"You are fed up with everything for the moment. And like the rest of us you are a little hungry for a little hope." This plea of one of the dope addicts in Jack Gelber's important play of 1957, *The Connection*, sounds a major theme of the postwar American theatre. For the dichotomy between pessimism and hope—between lamenting at the abyss and continuing to hang on to the edge of the precipice—has sharpened in the last two decades. Today's stage reflects this acute suffering, this crisis of hope.

Particular images of the dramatic tension between hope and hopelessness come immediately if one scans the American theatre panoramically: a frail young girl, blowing out the candles, who retreats again into her glass menagerie; a tired salesman whose suicidal death was motivated out of hope and despair; a Southern belle who wishes to ride a streetcar named desire until it crashes; a guilt-ridden family who quarrel each step of their long day's journey into night, and a young man who desperately tells a story about a zoo to a stranger in Central Park. Such images evoke the question which is the mark of much mid-twentieth-century literature, and which is dramatized, made real, on our stages: Wherein lies a man's hope? And that inquiry, of course, is a religious question, an ultimate question, one of those points at which religious and aesthetic considerations merge.

The dramatic movement of these plays therefore is not the classical and Elizabethan structure of falling and being raised up, but rather, a horizontal one, that of exile and alienation leading to the possibility of being restored. A fall as-

61

sumes something to fall from, something to suffer for, and something to be redeemed to. The modern imagination rejects this vertical metaphor, and, perhaps more analogous to the Genesis 3 account than we often suppose, portrays the experience of loss, of expulsion, of being shut out, of being excluded, of exile. Camus' diagnosis is as accurate for the American postwar theatre as it was for the literature of postwar Europe:

> In a universe that is suddenly deprived of illusions and of light, man feels a stranger. His is an irremediable exile, because he is deprived of memories of a lost homeland as much as he lacks the hope of a promised land to come.[1]

To hope is to take that complex stance of fear and expectancy, that ambiguous posture of doubt and faith at the same time. One loses hope when all his resources of meaning are cut off; an exile is he who is separated from that which gave purpose to his life. Alienated not only from God, but also from society and nature and sometimes even from himself, the protagonist in contemporary drama often attempts to engage in a quest to recover the lost connections. This search, religious in its intensity and significance, has pervaded the American theatre since World War II.

Gelber's play, *The Connection*, whose title suggested this explorative look at the religio-cultural aspects of American drama, richly interweaves the desperation and boredom of hope and hopelessness. In their Beat-Hippie pad, the young addicts are waiting for Cowboy, their connection, to bring them some dope. Or, is the connection really Leonard the Locomotive? One of them insists: "No, no. I mean the man behind them. I mean the big connection." For the play constantly is suggesting that the boys want more than dope; they want to be related to the ritual on the outside; they want a connection to meaning. Solly, in a burst of anger, confesses their longing:

[1]Albert Camus, *The Myth of Sisyphus*, trans. Justin O'Brien (New York: Vintage Books, 1959), p. 5.

You are fed up with everything for the moment. And like the rest of us you are a little hungry for a little hope. So you wait and worry. A fix of hope. A fix to forget. A fix to remember, to be sad, to be happy, to be, to be. So we wait for the trustworthy Cowboy to gallop in upon a white horse.

And that white horse, is it only the knight in shining armor, or is it, at the same time, the pale horse whose rider is death and destruction? For that which is to save them destroys them, and the characters live between the vague hope of "We are waiting. We have waited before. The connection is coming" and the realization, almost impossible to face, that "You are your own connection"—that each is condemned to be alone in his own anguish. Solly is right: the author, as he says, "has chosen this petty and miserable microcosm because of its self-annihilating aspects."

The attempt to recover lost connections, to gain a sense of hope, is pursued in this play, as it is in many other contemporary dramas, within dramatic actions of what now have often been cited as rituals and games. Ritual, the proscribed pattern of word, mime, and action, with its religious overtones, is found in the addicts' waiting for the dope, and especially in their receiving the shot and its effects. Game, with its spontaneity and improvisation, expresses itself in the jazz music and in the setting of the play as a rehearsal.

These two dramatic patterns have been a rediscovery of the roots of drama, and in our highly self-conscious age, knowledge of myth and psychological structures of meaning have given both the artists and the critics new insights into the nature of human actions. And in the last several decades of American drama, one can trace in microcosmic form the cyclic process of the use of these two patterns.

Ritual, the performance of meaningful actions related to larger social, political, or religious meanings, appears to be the first stage in the cycle. Through complacency and sheer habit, these actions degenerate into meaningless repetitions of dead and wooden practices without substance. Instead of commitment, there is only routine; instead of awe toward the larger whole, there is only indifference. The cyclic action moves towards game: spontaneous, improvisational, casual, experimental. One uses games, as Hamlet did, in order to recover meaning. The freedom is appealing; the adventure is exciting, and all is well until the very facile nature of game-playing becomes self-destructive. He who is playing a role becomes aware of the falsity of his role, of his mask-wearing. Instead of adventure, there is phoniness; instead of spontaneity, there are few, if any, directions or goals. He wants to be honest with himself and others. He wishes to remove the mask, but what is illusion and what is reality? If life is only a game, what is its value? What is the quality of one's life? In the masquerade, how does one get through to another? One of the main answers to this dilemma is found in groping to recover old rituals. And much of the avant-garde theatre of the late 1960s attempted to do just that.

Examining a number of the significant plays of the American theatre should provide a sensitive index of what is most deep and central in the fears and hopes of our generation.

— I —

If one wanted to discover an archetype of the image of man as connected, as related to time and space, no drama in the American tradition would be more appropriate than that of Thornton Wilder. A study entitled *The Theme of Loneliness in Modern American Drama* comments that Wilder

> seems to be something of an exception among playwrights in that whether he looks at the world in microcosm, as in *Our Town*, or in macrocosm, as in *The Skin of Our Teeth*, he sees man at home in his environment—without much margin to spare, it is true, but still at home and belonging.[2]

Especially in *Our Town* (1938), the role of man is understood to be part of a larger whole, a meaningful series of actions on the stage of the world. At the time of the play's first

---

[2]Winifred Dusenbury, *The Theme of Loneliness in Modern American Drama* (Gainesville: University of Florida Press, 1961), pp. 197–198.

production, Wilder suggested that "the central theme" of the play concerns "the relation between the countless 'unimportant' details of our daily life, on the one hand, and the great perspectives of time, social history and current religious ideas on the other."[3] Within the play itself, Rebecca speaks of an address in a letter, a list which many of us have doodled in the inside covers of our grade-school textbooks:

> *Jane Crofut; The Crofut Farm; Grover's Corners, Sutton County; New Hampshire; United States of America; Continent of North America; Western Hemisphere; the Earth; the Solar System; the Universe; the Mind of God—that's what it said on the envelope.*

The secure relationships therefore within the families of the Webbs and Gibbses, the banter and the gossip between the townspeople over the garden fences and at the church choir practice—all these point to the unifying harmony between man and his environment. For what binds the inhabitants of Grover's Corners to one another and to the eternities of time and space are the ritualistic actions in which they all participate. The arrival of the newsboy and the milkman, breakfast and its dishes, are repetitive patterns which give pleasure and meaning to their lives. More fundamentally, the cycle of birth, marriage, and death forms the major dramatic metaphor of the three acts of the play. The church choir in its two selections at George and Emily's wedding, "Love Divine, All Love Excelling," and "Blessed Be the Tie That Binds," sing of the physical, social, and spiritual harmonies which are operative in the lives of the townspeople. And the ending of the play is one of affirmation, for the Stage Manager possesses the perspective of meaningful patterns of existence:

> *Most everybody's asleep in Grover's Corners. There are a few lights on: Shorty Hawkins, down at the depot, has just watched the Albany train go by. And at the livery stable somebody's setting up late and talking. —Yes, it's clearing up. There are the stars—doing their old, old crisscross journeys in the sky.*

---

[3]Thornton Wilder, "Preface to *Our Town*," *The New York Times*, February 13, 1938.

Thus no basic incongruity marks Wilder's universe. The difficulties which the protagonist in Wilder's drama experiences are minor, for all is set against the backdrop of cosmic order and universal harmony. This awareness of order and harmony sustains him. He acknowledges therefore his involvement, with other men, with the past, and with God, for all these are but the manifestations of infinite purpose at work. This recognition of man's relatedness provides the source of identity and meaning.

Clearly, the mood of the play is nostalgic. Wilder set the play in 1901 in rural New Hampshire in order to catch a simpler environment with which man has to cope. Yet, the desire to create such a *communitas* is deep within us; in 1973, there were more than a thousand productions of *Our Town* in this country, and no play has been performed on high school stages more often than this one. Indeed, by participating in the miming and the rituals of *Our Town*, each audience is attempting, nostalgic as it may be, to recreate its connection to meaning and purpose.

— II —

In the crescendo climax of Tennessee Williams' play of 1947, *A Streetcar Named Desire*, Blanche Dubois is confronted by the ape-like vitality of her brother-in-law, Stanley Kowalski. She has lost everything; her family's estate, Belle Reve, has been sold; her husband committed suicide; her entire past as a Southern belle and a genteel school teacher is gone. She is alone and without any connections other than the nostalgic memories and past secrets which haunt her now. And when Stanley threatens, she goes for help to that modern device which connects one with another, the telephone: "Operator, operator! Give me long-distance, please. . . . I want to get in touch with Mr. Shep Huntleigh of Dallas." Perhaps Shep Huntleigh is only a fiction, a fantasy of the man on the white horse who will save her, yet Blanche places all her hope in him. She wants to get in touch, and she wants to send a message: "In desperate, desperate circumstances! Help me! Caught in a trap. Caught in—."

Blanche's message is precisely the one many of the men and women on American stages the last several decades would send. The world of Grover's Corners fell apart; its meaningful rituals, its tightly knit families and communal spirit have disintegrated. Instead, the characters in postwar American drama find themselves entangled in various snares, some of which they are helpless victims, others of which are mostly of their own doing. And these entanglements prevent them from having a significant relationship with sources of meaning.

One trap is a distorted awareness of the past, not as that which sustains and gives purpose to the present, as in Wilder's plays, but that which is a burden and condemns. The first play of the American postwar renaissance in drama, *The Glass Menagerie* (1944) dramatizes the ways in which the past paralyzes. Amanda, deep in her reveries of seventeen gentlemen callers in her youth, indulges in self-pity about her present life and imposes this bitterness upon her children. Tom, attempting to run from the unpleasant and impossible life in the confined apartment, discovers by the conclusion of the play, that all of the memories of that time and place are still with him. The past haunts him.

Brick, the protagonist in Williams' later play, *Cat on a Hot Tin Roof* (1955), is burdened by his past involvement with his best friend, Skipper. His relationship with his wife as well as with his entire family and himself, is frayed until the meaning of his relationship with Skipper is bared. His brooding, his drinking, and his surliness are all symptomatic escapes from the past.

If the core of Williams' drama often is to be found in the obsession with the past, the protagonists in several of Arthur Miller's plays are likewise enmeshed in past events which color their present. Joe Keller's (*All My Sons*, 1945) approval of faulty airplane parts in his factory and the subsequent condemnation of his business partner has gnawed him for years. Willy Loman's (*Death of a Salesman*, 1949) awareness that his son confronted him with another woman in a Boston hotel room has made all the difference in his relationship to his family for years. Quentin (*After the Fall*, 1964) is not only pursued by his own past shortcomings, but is overwhelmed with the guilt of the Jewish massacre of World War II. And, in

Miller's more recent play, *The Price* (1968), the two brothers who meet in the attic of the old family house, ostensibly to dispose of their father's belongings, actually are attempting to untangle their past relationships to him and to each other. Walter, the older brother, is savage in exposing the illusions which Victor has held:

> We invent ourselves, Vic, to wipe out what we know. You invent a life of self-sacrifice, a life of duty; but what never existed here cannot be upheld. You were not upholding something, you were denying what you knew they were. And denying yourself.

Walter finally confesses: "It is all an illusion and if we could walk through it, we could meet. . . ." But the brothers do not walk through it; they walk under it and around it, and therefore they lose their connection, their relationship to one another.

The motifs of the past and of illusions around which the drama of Williams and Miller centers loom large and find their roots in the writing of Eugene O'Neill. *Long Day's Journey into Night*, O'Neill's posthumous play published in 1955, is perhaps the archetypal portrayal of the loss of meaning based on the distorted perspective on the past. The Tyrone family ambivalently attempts to hide the painful events in their memories, but at the same time, they expose each other's past in cruel and hurting ways. The mother, Mary, when confronted with her attempt at suicide sometime ago, simply tries to place the event in fantasy: "It doesn't matter. Nothing like that ever happened. You must have dreamed it." In the very next speech, her husband, who a moment ago had reminded her of the suicide, bursts out: "Mary! For God's sake, forget the past!" And Mary, who by escaping into drug addiction lives in illusions greater than anyone else in the family, faces the matter directly: "Why? How can I? The past is present, isn't it? It's the future too. We all try to lie out of that, but life won't let us." Meanwhile, the fog descends on this home torn by intensity and pain, and the Tyrones are losing their relationships to one another. The oppressive fog has trapped them.

What has happened in many of these plays is that the

ritualistic actions in which Wilder's inhabitants of Grover's Corners participated, have lost their inner meaning and substance. Instead of the family meal being a ritualistic place of meeting and sharing, the table becomes either the area for quarreling, or, more likely, the non-meeting ground. Instead of the ritual of marriage symbolizing the unity of human love, it is exactly in that close relationship where the tensions are the greatest. Instead of finding one's identity and meaning in one's vocation, the very emptiness is reflected in the vacuity of work. And, instead of a meaningful death as the most significant ritualistic action which a man undergoes, the ambivalence of suicide marks the end of several of these dramatic protagonists.

What these people in O'Neill, Williams, and Miller have discovered is that by attempting to live in the past or to reject the past completely, they have created an illusion, a self-deception which haunts them. For living in illusion is certainly the most outstanding trap in which these people are caught. Since they are not their true and whole selves but rather are false and incomplete, they cannot be in touch with their world. The impersonal relationship between man and his environment, and the cutting off of one person from another, even within his own family, points toward the loss of connection to meaning and purpose. The inhabitants of Grover's Corners believe; they accept as truth the destiny of their lives. The people in O'Neill, Williams, and Miller experience uncertainty and doubt, even despair. They have lost their faith in God, in each other, and sometimes even in themselves.

— III —

If disbelief and unbelief be dominant, then what? Ritual is dead, what next? Let's "make" believe, let's imagine, let's pretend, let's suspend disbelief. Ritual is dead; long live the game. If the prescribed pattern with its incantation of words and its use of appropriate mime which marks ritual has lost its substance, then the other axis of dramatic action may be exploited, that of spontaneity and improvisation. For the action is play; the people are players, and in deliberately and self-consciously playing a role, they, like Hamlet, may be given insight into knowing what is their destiny. By putting on masks for a temporary interval, the perspective of distance and the final unmasking may reveal the actualities underneath. They may then be able to get through to each other and to themselves. They possibly may recover their connection.

Several major plays of the 1960s document the use of games, of deliberate improvisational role-playing, in order to recover meaning and purpose in one's existence. One of the most well known is Albee's *Who's Afraid of Virginia Woolf?* (1962). The echoes of the child's ditty, "Who's afraid of the big, bad wolf?" sung to the tune of "The Mulberry Bush," blend into the major action of the drama: the playing of games, games of childhood and games of fantasy. In the first act, "Fun and Games," the game is on George, "Humiliate the Host." His failure as a scholar and as a person is exposed; in Martha's words: "He's in a bog!" Nick is at the center of the second game, "Hump the Hostess." His "wave-of-the-future" opportunism is shown for what it is when he admits that he has married Honey only for wealth and convenience, and that he is impotent in his seduction of Martha. A quick game comes next, "Get the Guests." Honey's (her syrupy sentimentality is as artificial as Nick's suave coolness, which is actually callowness) eagerness to have children and her inability to do so, make sterility, physical and spiritual, once more a major theme of the play. The final game is the most serious: "Bringing Up Baby." George now announces that the son whom Martha constantly mentions is merely a fantasy which they have created to compensate for their inability to have children. Martha therefore reaches her sad moment of truth when she confesses in the last line that she, in contrast to her earlier bluster, is indeed afraid of Virginia Woolf. The tune that had been such a humorous success at the party earlier in the evening has been transformed, by its melody of "The Mulberry Bush," into a fading whimper of the Hollow Men. For each of the four has realized that their illusions have hidden truth, that only by unmasking can there be self-knowledge.

Albee, in an interview in 1965, when queried why it is

that the characters in his plays seem so bent on tearing each other apart, answered: "I suppose the characters in my plays are interested in teaching other characters about self-knowledge."[4] For, in the course of the play, each character, his inhibitions slowly drained by alcohol, begins to bare his gangrenous soul. Each gradually reveals that the appearance he presents to society is a mask for the hideous truth, the grisly wolf of the title. Each, through the playing of games, has been confronted with the raw truth of his or her past existence. In the titles of the three acts of the play, the dramatic movement has been from Fun and Games through the orgies of Walpurgisnacht to the Exorcism, a ritualistic action to purge and to free all of them from the evil spirits of past illusions. In the soft whispers into which the play modulates at its conclusion, George and Martha, if only temporarily, have achieved a relationship of understanding and forgiving love.

The Boys in the Band (1968), Mart Crowley's drama, is also concerned with the breaking down of pretenses, with the acceptance of reality. Just as in Albee's play, the wit is cruel and excoriating. The subject of the play is a group of homosexuals, but the significance of the drama is totally human and universal. And at the center of the play is a savage game called "Affairs of the Heart."

The occasion is a birthday party for Harold, by his own description, "a thirty-two-year-old, ugly, pock-marked Jew fairy." The deep anguish and guilt-ridden inside of each of the guests is glossed over by a jesting and extremely facile wit which at times becomes almost a parody of itself:

MICHAEL: *What are you so depressed about? I mean other than the usual everything.*

DONALD: *I really don't want to get into it.*

MICHAEL: *Well, if you're not going to tell me, how can we have a conversation in depth—a warm, rewarding, meaningful friendship?*

These two friends, as all the others, do genuinely desire to get through to each other, but their isolation overwhelms them.

---

[4]Cited in *The Playwrights Speak*, ed. Walter Wager (New York: Dell Publishing, 1967), p. 47.

No one is going to permit himself to feel anything; the risks are too high.

Michael, the host of the evening, particularly to hide his own pain, resorts to playing games with the secret, carefully overlaid, torments of his friends. The game, a bit too patly adopted from *Virginia Woolf*, is introduced as "a combination of both the Truth Game and Murder—with a new twist." Everyone present is to telephone someone he has loved unrequitedly; he will be given points for each open declaration he makes during the conversation. The shield of private humor is no longer enough; group exposure will now take place. All drunk by now, the party-goers guzzle this witch's brew of truth. In the midst of his anguished hysterics, Michael stammers: ". . . if we . . . if we could just . . . not hate ourselves so much. That's it you know. If we could just *learn* not to hate ourselves quite so very much." The guests all drift out, and Michael again retreats into his flippancy, but all have experienced one moment of truth, one moment of awareness of what their communion in the same human agony implies. For an instant, in the middle of the game playing, they have a connection with truth and to one another.

The process of communication, the attempt to arrive at communion, to gain a connection with another and one's self, by means of games and improvisational role-playing—this was central in many dramas of the early 1960s. One of the American plays already firmly placed in many anthologies, Edward Albee's *The Zoo Story* (1958), dramatizes the use of language and gesture from good-natured kidding around to a climax of violence approaching an almost animalistic nature. This process one can discover in many other plays of the 1960s: William Hanley's *Slow Dance on the Killing Ground* (1964) and the plays of LeRoi Jones, *The Toilet* (1963) and *Dutchman* (1964). In each of these plays, after a period of talk and game-playing, physical violence erupts, and out of the violence comes, if not self-renewal and knowledge, an exhausted purgation of the extremely hostile feelings which were the major obstacles to meaningful meeting before the confrontation. Out of this frenzied trauma comes a communication in many of these plays which is deep and significant.

— IV —

In the last phase of the cycle from ritual through game and back to ritual is the most controversial area of contemporary drama: the Radical Theatre Repertory. This rather amorphously organized group of some dozen and a half acting ensembles, located mostly in New York, includes Joseph Chaikin's Open Theatre, Richard Schechner's Performance Group, Jerzy Grotowski's Polish Laboratory Theatre, and the most well-known of them all, the Living Theatre of Julian Beck and Judith Malina. To explore the ritualistic nuances of the work of these theatres is to perceive something of both the cultural and religious expressions of our time.

According to the program sheet for *Mysteries and Smaller Pieces* (1968), one of the Living Theatre's productions, all of these groups in the Sixties saw themselves

> in the vanguard of a new phenomenon in theatrical and social history—the spontaneous generation of communal playing troups, sharing voluntary poverty, making experimental collective creations and utilizing space, time, minds and bodies in manifold new ways that meet the demands of our explosive period.

It is theatre which is largely stripped of narrative, even of words; it is theatre which expresses itself in sound and movement—writhing, yoga exercises, breathing, chants, frenzied howls and screams—for the body is the center of the action.

This emphasis on physicality has been present from the very beginning of the movement. Kenneth Brown, author of *The Brig*, which, with *The Connection*, were the Living Theatre's first productions, described his play as "an indictment of the senses in order to reach the soul."[5] The use of the body, in exercises and sometimes in nudity, is the way in which the actors insist that they arrive at an Artaudian vision of "total awareness." Such people see physical theatre as an

---

[5]Cited in Richard Schechner, "Interviews with Judith Malina and Kenneth H. Brown," *Tulane Drama Review*, VIII (Spring, 1964), 213.

effective method of removing the false masks, of stopping the role-playing, and of attempting to reveal honesty and integrity. Elsa Gress is certainly accurate in calling this tendency "body-romanticism," and she comments that "romanticists are always hankering for the ineffable,"[6] a statement which perceptively suggests the religious framework of the entire movement.

In varying degrees, many of the new theatres are communities. Grotowski speaks of his theatrical people as "novitiates" and "disciples." The Open Theatre and the Performance Group believe that life-style and performing style are not separable, and Schechner adds: "You simply cannot be a great performer and a lousy human being."[7] The Living Theatre acknowledges that its followers are cultic in their devotion, according to an interview by Judith Malina:

> People come to travel with us. And they say, 'I'm going to go with you no matter what you say to me.' And we say, 'Please, don't do this to us.' And they say, 'I don't care, I'm going to be there.' And then they walk across the Alps in the winter and they follow us and they hitchhike and they hustle and they God-knows-what to stay with us and to follow us from city to city. . . .[8]

New York Times critic Walter Kerr puts it succinctly: "The majority of the performers do not seem to be actors at all. They are converts."[9]

Not only do the actors view themselves as a community, but the audience itself becomes a participating community. One critic describes the relationship of actors to audience as

[6]Elsa Gress, "Ohorganism: The Lost Years," *The Drama Review*, XIII (Spring, 1969), 118.

[7]Schechner, "Want to Watch? Or Act?" *The New York Times*, January 12, 1969.

[8]Cited in Schechner, "Containment Is the Enemy," *The Drama Review*, XIII (Spring, 1969), 36.

[9]Walter Kerr, "You Will Not Be Lonely," *The New York Times*, October 6, 1968.

one of "priests to catechumens,"[10] and an actor points out the resemblance of the Living Theatre to the Old Time Religion:

> When you 'get it' you stand up and shout and roll about. Such enthusiasm, without apparent reason . . . can seem funny to you if you watch it. But if you try it you risk conversion, because it's fun. Physically celebratory religion is one way to make yourself feel whole.[11]

Involvement and participation are the key concepts; the actors and the audience, if the ritual has been meaningful, agree that they have undergone an experience. They have been connected to each other and to meaning.

Paradise Now (1968) is the most elaborate work in the repertoire of the Living Theatre that I have experienced. Within the pseudo-classical architecture of the Brooklyn Academy of Music with its high ceiling and opera seats, a group of actors desperately attempted to engage us in a ritualistic celebration. While taking the mystical voyage up the eight rungs of Hebrew and Indian philosophy described on the 17-by-22-inch "map" for the evening, the actors often engaged in either small clusters of confrontation politics within the auditorium or in group gropes of love piles on the stage. The chanting liturgical litanies and the ceremonial gestures of the actors all became what the map called "collective creation." The designation of the seven rungs indicated the journey (the map described it as "the voyage from the many to the one") on which the participants embarked: the Rung of Good and Evil, the Rung of Prayer, the Rung of Teaching, the Rung of the Way, the Rung of Redemption, the Rung of Love, the Rung of Heaven and Earth, the Rung of God and Man. For me, the climactic moment came at the eighth rung ("the Rite of I and Thou") when the performers began to scream at each other: "Black! White! Old! Young! Christian! Jew!" They

[10]Stefan Brecht, "Revolution at the Brooklyn Academy of Music," *The Drama Review*, XIII (Spring, 1969), 64.
[11]Patrick McDermott, "Portrait of an Actor, Watching," *The Drama Review*, XIII (Spring, 1969), 80.

then turned their name-calling on the audience. Finally, softly and slowly, the chant began: "I. Thou." Their symbolism, as one actor-critic points out, is

> a step beyond the images at work in the 'lines' of a play delivered by one actor to another. They test their commitment to Buber's principles by rubbing them between their own flesh and the flesh of strangers.[12]

The people of Living Theatre wish to engage in meeting; they desire to find, with us, the loss of connection.

The major impression of the evening was the desperate attempt of the actors to get through—to audience, to meaning itself, to Paradise. As Beck has said, "Here we are, locked outside of the gates of Paradise,"[13] and this feeling of exile, of disconnection, motivates the participants to reach and touch one another in the search for what Judith Malina describes as "the uncorrupted part of Eden."[14]

It is therefore not surprising that several of the most significant titles in the Radical Theatre repertory revolve about the quest for Paradise. Schechner's *Dionysus in 69* (1969), with its rituals of birth and celebrations of dance, reinterpreted Euripides' *Bacchae* as the process by which one finds meaning and peace. To be Dionysion is not only to engage in a pagan and orgiastic frenzy, but also to find what it means to be at one with each other and the universe.

The Serpent (1969), Jean-Claude van Itallie's exploration of the book of Genesis performed by the Open Theatre, "aspires to the most holy (and fundamental) theatrical impulse," according to critic John Lahr, for it intends "to return the actors and the audience to an intuition of the primordial state."[15] All of the reenactments of the biblical narratives, and especially the Garden sequence, are designed to embody prelapsarian innocence. The author's comments in the introduction to the play also speak of

---

[12]*Ibid.*, p. 76.
[13]Cited in Schechner, "Containment Is the Enemy," p. 29.
[14]*Ibid.*, p. 26.
[15]John Lahr, *Up Against the Fourth Wall: Essays on the Modern Theatre* (New York: Grove Press, 1970), p. 160.

the theatre's uniquely important advantage and function, its original religious function of bringing people together in a community ceremony where the actors are in some sense priests or celebrants, and the audience is drawn to participate with the actors in a kind of eucharist.

As in *Paradise Now*, the entire ceremonial ritual is held in order to celebrate creation, but still more, recreation, not in the sense of entertainment, but of renewing one's relationship with one's fellowmen and with nature.

Jerzy Grotowski's Polish Laboratory Theatre, although not strictly American, has nevertheless had more influence on American radical theatre than any other group. His drama, *Apocalypsis cum Figuris* (1969), recently performed several times in this country, also, according to the program notes, "evolved from acting exercises and improvisations." Grotowski insists that, "despite the title, this production is not a dramatization of the Revelation of St. John." But the names of the characters—Simon Peter, John, Judas, Mary Magdalene, Lazarus—and their reenactment (although Grotowski repudiates this term) of several Gospel narratives indicates the biblical counterpoint within the drama. Grotowski's description of the main character, the Simpleton who is assigned the role of Christ, reveals the drama's communal ritual: "an innocent, gullible half-wit, living outside the accepted conventions, gawkish, often deformed, but in mysterious communion with the supernatural." Such a figure is related to the demonaic and the village idiot in the Slavic tradition, as Grotowski suggests, but also to the Fool in our literary conventions. The Simpleton, foolish by society's standards, is a fool for Christ in his innocence and total giving of self to others.

The story of the play is thus the story of Christ, but in the words of a perceptive Polish commentator on the play, the myth has been ferociously "vivisected":

> The Christ myth is subjected to the test of blasphemy, the test of cynicism, and the test of verbal argumentation, the most acute ever made, since it comes from *The Brothers Karamazov*. The object is to strip the myth of all the rich finery in which it

has been decked out by religion, tradition, and habit: to have it stand naked before us and try to defend itself.[16]

The participant, one should add, also stands naked before the action, and he finds that he too is confronted with the truth dramatized in the ritual.

Again, as in much of this theatre, the experience of the performance of *Apocalypsis* is much more than the text one reads. Inaccessible (the company's home is an obscure Polish city, Wroclaw, and the group seldom travels) and limited (no performance admits more than a hundred people, usually forty or fifty), Grotowski's theatre came to Philadelphia for a short time in Fall, 1973. The setting chosen was itself appropriate: the abandoned and cavernous St. Alphonsus Church in South Philadelphia. The audience gathered in the basement of the church (there was no admission charge); almost all were college age since the announcement had said only students would be admitted. The audience, some sitting in loosely arranged chairs, some standing, smoking, chattering, waited. By all the laws of logic, this should have been irritating. Instead, the mood became sociable and open. Waiting for Grotowski already formed the basis for a community.

A few minutes before performance time, the audience, ten or so at a time, was led up a narrow back stairway to the main sanctuary, which was totally empty and almost dark. Absolute silence. Seated on the floor, the entire group was formed into one large circle, and the discomfort of the setting served to make one still more aware of one's body. A single spotlight pointed across the space up to the ceiling, on which there was a painting of Christ's coronation in heaven. But Christ the King was not the subject of this presentation. Rather it was the Body of Christ, Christ the victim of a sacrificial ritual and of humanity.

In one of the sequences, Mary Magdalene began to murmur softly, her voice gradually rising until one heard she was singing something in Spanish. The words are repeated by

---

[16]Konstanty Puzyna, "A Myth Vivisected: Grotowski's *Apocalypse*," *The Drama Review*, XV (Fall, 1971), 38.

John: "Verily, verily, I say unto you, except ye eat the flesh of the Son of Man, and drink his blood, ye have no life in you. For my flesh is meat indeed, and my blood is drink indeed." While this litany was being chanted, the others crowded in on the Simpleton, pulled away his black peasant's coat, and bit at his body. Such an action, blasphemous as it first appears, at the same time, recreates the holy. The participant is confronted with astonishing rituals: His body was crucified and torn, and I am still tearing it apart each day; my very life is sustained and nourished by the body and blood of Christ.

The setting, the action, the response all confirmed that drama as a genre is inherently involved in the religious, both historically and thematically (which is one reason why the church and the theatre have almost always been in controversy—it is a family quarrel, for each knows it is not really complete without the other.) But modern drama has been much more blatant about the way in which the theatre assumes the function of a substitute church. George Bernard Shaw's famous statement that "the theater is really the weekday church" was echoed by Gordon Craig, the influential producer-playwright of the early twentieth century: "Art is not a pick-me-up; it is a communion. . . . The theater is not a bar; it is a famous temple." The theatre and its near relative, the movie palace, have become the place where men congregate to experience deep insights and to find meaning for their lives. For, in an unmagical world in which many men see no spirit at work other than their own, the theatre will be viewed as a temple, and within its ritualistic actions, men will seek to participate in the cosmic drama.

A performance such as *Apocalypsis* has made drama transcendent once more; as in the Greek and Elizabethan tragedies, such a theatre, in the root sense of "apocalypse," reveals, uncovers. The actors with their expressive backs, eloquent necks, and powerful feet presented a work of pure body which at the same time manifested itself as a dimension of the spiritual. The revelation and uncovering bared the inner soul; the audience departed in complete silence, having participated in a ritual of both the passion of man and the passion of God.

— V —

Alan Watts[17] has pointed out that the most basic model or image of the world which has governed Western civilization has been the idea of the universe as a political monarchy. Such an idea underlies the biblical imagery, and therefore in the Jewish, Islamic, and Christian traditions, the universe is viewed as a system of order which is ruled by spiritual force from above.

The second great model, Watts goes on to suggest, is the image of the world as machine. The controller, the personal God has disappeared, and one is simply left with the machine. It is all a completely mindless mechanical process whose principles are to be explained by analogy with the game of billiards.

The way in which modern man is trying to make sense out of reality, Watts finally describes, is through the image of the world as a body, an organism. The universe is understood as a vast pattern of intelligent energy which has a new relationship to us. Watts elaborates:

> We are not in it [the world] as subjects of a king, nor as victims of a blind process. We are not *in* it at all. We *are* it! It's you! Every individual in this organic myth of the world must look upon himself as responsible for the world.

In the words of the title of Stanley Burnshaw's significant book, man is a "seamless web" of relationships.[18] Not only ecologists but also artists and philosophers are reminding us that the organic relationship between man and man, between man and his world, is needed in order to meet our crisis of hope.

"Only connect!" wrote E. M. Forster in the first decade of this century. This stage direction, we are attempting to understand and to follow.

---

[17]Alan Watts, "Mythological Roots of Modern Science," *Directions* 6, pp. 6–9, a publication of the Society for the Arts, Religion, and Contemporary Culture.

[18]Stanley Burnshaw, *The Seamless Web* (New York: Braziller, 1970).

§ FIVE §

PIPE DREAMS AND ALCOHOL:
In Vino Veritas

The theme of reality and illusion has long been recognized as inherent in drama. The use of mask, whether literal or metaphorical, for example, indicates the essence of drama: the relationship between what is actual and what is illusory. The etymology of the word "illusion" (to play) provides a further clue to dramatic action, for the audience in the *theatron* (the place of seeing, of beholding) is being confronted with direct questions: Is Oedipus really blind? Is Iago actually honest? Is the waiting of Gogo and Didi an illusion? The effect is double: not only is the character caught between what he believes to be true and what really is, but the spectator also must attempt to sort out appearances from actualities. Dramatist, actors, and audience are all involved in a complex playing with reality.

One strand of the traditional theme of reality and illusion, found particularly in post-World War II American drama, is the dramatic device of alcoholic drunkenness. Eugene O'Neill, in this as in many other American dramatic themes and techniques, is undoubtedly the father of this approach, with Tennessee Williams, Edward Albee, Jason Miller, and several other dramatists providing variations on the many-sided topic. This chapter will explore how these playwrights have, with acumen and perceptivity, expanded and redirected the conventional conflict of reality and illusion, both as setting (an atmosphere of alcohol) and as point of view (one or more characters on stage who are drunk).

— *I* —

The settings for the atmosphere of alcohol are, of course, sometimes bars. In plays as diverse as Saroyan's *The Time of Your Life,* O'Neill's *The Iceman Cometh,* and Charles Gordone's black play *No Place to Be Somebody,* the saloon location sets both tone and character motivation in action. More frequently, however, the setting is within a home, such as the living room in the plays of O'Neill and Albee or the coach's cottage in *That Championship Season.*

The particular setting is less important for the dramatic action than what the characters wish to create as their milieu. The characters have gathered, no matter what their actual location, to find mutual community, to participate in a ritual of openness and togetherness. Dionysius remains since the beginnings of drama as the god to be worshipped in the partaking of sacramental food and wine. To be enthusiastic, that is, to be filled with a god, is the purpose of gathering to construct, however temporary, a Utopia. In such a kingdom, good will is nurtured by alcohol; each citizen is tolerant of his neighbor's illusions. Thus the bars are significantly named: Harry Hope's Saloon in O'Neill's *The Iceman Cometh,* and the Pacific Street Saloon in Saroyan's *The Time of Your Life.* The goal is life, to enjoy life together forever, to find the time of your life.

Although the attempt is made to recreate a heaven, a state of hellishness is frequently the result. Instead of participating in ritual community, each character experiences deep loneliness. The saloon dwellers feel intoxicated, that is, filled with a poison, or as Hickey says with bravado in *Iceman:* "Bring on the rat poison!" Hope and peace may be the names of the saloons, but at least one character in *Iceman* perceives the true nature of the setting:

> *It's the No Chance Saloon. It's Bedrock Bar, the End of the Life Cafe, the Bottom of the Sea Rathskeller! Don't you notice the beautiful calm in the atmosphere? That's because it's the last harbor. No one here has to worry about where they're going next, because there is no farther they can go.*

Depressed, overwhelmed with guilt and self-pity, the characters frequently experience a slow dying, for each is losing the time of his life.

And yet the participants continue to come and continue to drink, for the atmosphere of alcohol encourages them to forget the past and to dream of the future. Both the past and the future are recreated in a haze, and the daydreams about the future frequently end in a nightmare, and the ideals about the future frequently lead to more illusions. Blanche Dubois in *A Streetcar Named Desire* desperately needs, as the play indicates, Southern Comfort, but it does not provide true relief for her. Martha in *Who's Afraid of Virginia Woolf?* admits "I'm firsty," but her deep longings are not fulfilled by her cravings for gin. "This dump is the Palace of Pipe Dreams!" Larry Slade perceptively notes in *Iceman*. In *Long Day's Journey into Night*, the sons play the game of "Watering Father's Whiskey Bottle," but the illusion is intensified by the fact that the sons know their father is aware of their deception. And he knows they know he knows it. They, as well as many others, are aware, however vaguely, that fantasies are both the blessing and the curse of their alcoholic consumption.

The process of entering the world of illusion is often gradual, yet inevitable. George in *Virginia Woolf* describes the first step: "I'm numbed enough... and I don't mean by liquor, though maybe that's been part of the process—a gradual, over-the-years going to sleep of the brain cells...." After numbness comes sleep, for then one can avoid the present by peacefully dreaming. But the inevitable result is what *Iceman's* Slade characterizes as "the peace of death." Hickey adds that "the waiting for the Big Sleep is a pipe dream." Waiting for the expectant future, for the big break, becomes the main action in such a setting, as it does for two characters in Saroyan's play:

> JOE: *Now, why do I drink? Why does anybody drink? Every day has twenty-four hours.*
>
> MARY: *Yes, that's true.*
>
> JOE: *Twenty-four hours. Out of the twenty-four hours at least twenty-three and a half are—my God, I don't know why—*

> dull, dead, boring, empty, and murderous. Minutes on the clock,
> not time of living. It doesn't make any difference who you are
> or what you do, twenty-three and a half hours of the twenty-
> four are spent waiting.

MARY: *Waiting?*

JOE: *And the more you wait, the less there is to wait for.*

MARY: *Oh?*

JOE: *That goes on for days and days, and weeks and months and
years, and years, and the first thing you know all the years are
dead. . . . There's nothing to wait for any more. Nothing except*
minutes on the clock. No time of life.

Time is the villain in the setting of alcoholic haze, and
therefore Edmund gives advice in *Long Day's Journey* as he
recites a translation of Baudelaire's poetry:

> Be always drunken. Nothing else matters: that is the only question.
> If you would not feel the horrible burden of Time weighing on your
> shoulders and crushing you to the earth, be drunken continually.

Martha (*Who's Afraid of Virginia Woolf?*) described the
continued recycling of grief and suffering in a striking image:

> I cry alllll the time; but deep inside, so no one can see me. I cry all
> the time. And Georgie cries all the time, too. We both cry all the
> time, and then, what we do, we cry, and we take our tears, and we
> put 'em in the ice box in the goddam ice trays until they're all frozen
> and then. . . we put them. . . in our. . . drinks.

One thinks of Dante's Satan, caught in the frozen lake of
Cocytus, the cold air generated by his own desperate wing-
flapping.

Yet the alcoholic setting is not always the Inferno. The
very presence of booziness may provide a purgatory, a cleansing of the memories of the past and of the hopes of the future
by facing the reality of the present.

Jamie in *Long Day's Journey,* having stumbled into the
house after his all-night binge on the town, speaks directly
and frankly to Edmund about his own jealousy and love for his
brother. He insists that what he is saying is "not drunken bull,
but 'in vino veritas' stuff. You better take it seriously. Want to

warn you—against me." Jamie concludes: "Greater love hath
no man than this, that he saveth his brother from himself.
(*Very drunkenly, his head bobbing.*) That's all. Feel better now.
Gone to confession." Out of the depths of his depression and
lubricated by the alcohol, Jamie is completely open. He has
undergone a purging of illusion and is finally confronting himself with the reality of the family's desperate situation.

—*II*—

Not only atmosphere and setting is affected by the presence of
alcohol within a play, but also point of view becomes more
direct than usual in drama when a character on stage is drunk.
Such a character often performs a choric function within the
dramatization, for he becomes both ideal spectator and bridge
between audience and stage. In the state of drunkenness, such
a character sees perceptively the ironies and contradictions
which the others on stage are hiding or avoiding. He is both
aware and unaware of his truth-conveying, for he often speaks
better than he knows. Both the audience and the other
characters frequently laugh at him, but his outrageous comments expose the illusions under which all are masking the truth.

Such a description reminds one not only of the drunken
porter in *Macbeth*, but also of two conventional figures within
the dramatic tradition. The prophet-seer in Greek tragedy and
the fool in medieval and Elizabethan drama are perhaps part of
the ancestral heritage of this particular character in post-
World War II drama in this country. While others on stage
regard such a figure as mad and insane, he is actually a genius,
both in the root sense of *genii* (filled with an elemental spirit
who influences another for good or evil) and in the more usual
sense of a person endowed with mental superiority. In his
ambivalent moods of depression and high frenzy, he reveals to
the audience, to others on stage, and sometimes even to himself, the dimensions of dream and nightmare, illusion and
reality. As Larry Slade comments at the beginning of *Iceman*:
"The lie of a pipe dream is what gives life to the whole mis-
begotten mad lot of us, drunk or sober. And that's enough

philosophic wisdom to give you for one drink of rot-gut." The next speaker calls Slade "de old Follosopher," and Slade has indicated in an earlier speech that the gathering at Harry Hope's Saloon is "The Feast of All Fools." In his drunkenness, such a character plays with reality, and in that playing, he exposes us to the multi-dimensionality of human motivation.

Tom in Williams' *Glass Menagerie,* in a scene similar to the scene with Jamie in *Long Day's Journey,* has only one time in which he, in his drunkenness, faces directly the illusions of the Wingfield family. Coming home drunk on Kentucky Straight Bourbon which the magician had given him for assisting in his stage show, Tom speaks of both his and Laura's dilemma of being trapped: "You know it don't take much intelligence to get yourself into a nailed-up coffin, Laura. But who in hell ever got himself out of one without removing one nail?" But Tom never again is drunk on stage, and to the end of the play, he continues to live in illusion.

"Never mix—never worry" is Honey's opening remark in *Who's Afraid of Virginia Woolf?* Nick's young wife does not mix her brandy as the night progresses, but she does have worries: Nick's unfaithfulness and her own fears of pregnancy. Her inane repetition of the remarks of others betrays her naive unawareness of what is actually happening in the house of George and Martha. As she says, "I peel labels," but unlike George, she does not "get down to the bone . . . the marrow." Honey and brandy: the mix remains sweet and syrupy; Honey confronts very little, if any, straight truth.

Three plays in recent American theater include a drunk character who during the entire play becomes one of the major points of view through which much of the action is filtered and reflected.

Hugo, the one-time editor of Anarchist periodicals who inhabits Harry Hope's saloon in *The Iceman Cometh,* spends most of the time in the bar in a dazed sleep, but when he arouses himself, he calls the others "monkey-faces" and tells them to "laugh like fools, leedle stupid people." He adds: "I vill laugh, too! But I vill laugh last! I vill laugh at you!" Most of all, he repeats his prophetic warning again and again: "The days grow hot, O Babylon! 'Tis cool beneath the villow trees!"

By the end of Act III, Hugo incisively confesses that his wisdom should not be heeded:

> *Please, for Gott's sake! I am not trunk enough! I cannot sleep! Life is a crazy monkey-face! Always there is blood beneath the villow trees! I hate it and I am afraid!* (He hides his face on his arms, sobbing muffedly.) *Please, I am crazy trunk! I say crazy things! For Gott's sake, do not listen to me!*

And, ironically, no one pays attention to him. In the last act, Hugo has come full circle; now he denounces Hickey for attempting to have all the habitués face the truth: "I'm glad, Larry, they take the crazy Hickey away to asylum. He makes me have bad dreams. He makes me tell lies about myself. He makes me want to spit on all I have ever dreamed." Appropriately, Hugh concludes the play singing the French Revolutionary "Carmagrole" with drunken fervor, still calling the others "stupid bourgeois monkeys." All join to "*shout in enthusiastic jeering chorus:* 'The days grow hot, O Babylon! 'Tis cool beneath the willow trees!'" All are roaring with laughter, and Hugo giggles with them. As leader of the chorus, Hugh both reflects the communal illusions and symbolizes the point of view which the play dramatizes: living in loneliness by nurturing each other's individual pipe dreams.

Albee in *A Delicate Balance* develops the character of Claire, vodka-drinking sister of Agnes, the head of the household who keeps the family in its fragile equilibrium. With wit and cynicism, Claire perceives that

> *We can't have changes—throws the balance off. Just think, Tobias, what would happen if the patterns changed: you wouldn't know where you stood, and the world would be full of strangers; that would never do.*

But the world is full of strangers, not only the neighbors Harry and Edna, but also sisters, daughters, husbands, and wives who are strangers to one another. Claire herself recognizes the advantage of her perspective: "Sidelines! Good seats, right on the fifty-yard line, objective observer." Agnes admits that "Claire is the strongest of us all: the walking wounded often are the least susceptible. . . ." Part of the reason for Claire's strength is her ability to face herself. While the others should change and do not, Claire perceptively acknowledges that to leave her alcoholism would be "the first step" in a spectrum of painfulness: "Sanity, insanity, revelation, self-deception . . .," and therefore Claire remains as she is: "My name is Claire, and I am an alcoholic." When Agnes's husband calls Claire "a great damn fool," she accepts it. Agnes later adds another characteristic of the fool: "If you are not an alcoholic, you are beyond forgiveness." The others on stage tolerate Claire as they would a court fool; they often regard her as harmless and amusing, and they forgive her when she chides them. But all are subconsciously aware that she is telling them what they need to know: the truth about themselves. Agnes articulates this need directly:

> *Claire could tell us so much if she cared to, could you not, Claire. Claire, who watches from the sidelines, has seen so very much, has seen us all so clearly, have you not, Claire. You were not named for nothing.*

Claire is bright; she sees the truth with clarity.

The 1972 prize-winning play, *That Championship Season*, dramatizes a final character whose point of view contrasts the world of truth with the world of illusion, the world in which the coach and the players are still living, twenty years after their state high school basketball championship. Tom Daley, feisty in his satirical comments about the falsity of the others, is called by his own brother: "You're nothing but a . . . complete and total disgrace. All cheap cynicism and booze." The coach remarks after one of Tom's biting truths that "you've been sneering at us all night. Laughing in our faces." Honesty with self (he calls himself "an alkie" and admits he is sick), his insistence that the others stop lying to one another, and most of all, his simple directness ("We are a myth" and are living in "the past tense")—all these characteristics lead to the coach's command for Tom to get out, an action analogous to Oedipus's denouncement of Tiresias, Lear's banishment of his fool, and Falstaff's departure from Prince Hal. For the prophet-seer and the fool cannot be tolerated in a false society. In the midst of Tom's earlier pathetic drunken fall from the steps, he presented his message: "My friends, I leave you with these words of wisdom. In the kingdom of the blind . . . the one-eyed man is king." Tom's drunkenness makes him blind to much, but within the kingdom of almost total darkness in which the others are living, Tom's insights make him not only lowly fool, but also give him the status of king.

— III —

The atmosphere of alcohol and the presence of a drunk character within postwar American drama both rely on the past tradition of theatre as well as expand and redirect that tradition.

English stage comedy, especially in Oscar Wilde and Noel Coward, found cocktails an appropriate lubricant to encourage the chatter and light banter of the dialogue. In Chekhov's *Cherry Orchard,* champagne is served at the departure from the family estate, a nostalgic celebration filled with emptiness. American theatre is perhaps closer to a play such as Gorki's *Lower Depths,* for here too one has a panoramic view of society, each individual able neither to forget nor to rid himself of guilt and failure. Such people are not content with champagne and cocktail-sipping, but in desperation enter a hazed alcoholic stupor. The heavy reliance on alcohol becomes both cause and symptom of their desperate state. The dreams and illusions fostered by the atmosphere of alcohol are a dramatic means of conveying and heightening realism.

A second reason for the dominant presence of alcohol in recent American plays may be attributed, paradoxically, to an attempt to break through photographic realism. Much of the postwar European drama rejected Ibsen's living room settings, and in plot, character, and dialogue moved into the absurd. The irrational, the grotesque, the bizarre—these are the marks of much of the Continental theater which reflected the metaphysical anguish in response to meaninglessness.

But the American theatre has generally embraced neither the presuppositions nor the techniques of the Theater of the Absurd. Exceptions such as Albee's *American Dream,* which shows debts to Ionesco's *Bald Soprano,* and John Guare's *The House of Blue Leaves,* which possesses a ridiculous zaniness, are nevertheless set within a realistic framework. American drama neither conveys the sense of nothingness present in Beckett and Genet, nor does it believe human communication is as difficult and as impossible as Ionesco and Pinter have dramatized it.

Instead, American drama has portrayed the acute suffering and anxiety of mid-twentieth century man within the framework of realism. But the devices of the atmosphere of alcohol and the drunk character have added a dimension to this realism, for through the use of these devices, the quest for meaning often ends in a greater illusion. And, though the quest frequently results in deep loneliness, nevertheless the hope is to find companionship and communal happiness, a heaven on earth.

Tom Wingfield, Blanche Dubois, the inhabitants of both the Pacific Street and Harry Hope's Saloons, the Tyrone family, the foursome at George and Martha's party, Claire, and Tom Daley—all of these characters in their various states of drunkenness play with reality, and in watching them do so, we once again behold the dramatic possibilities of one of the theatre's oldest struggles: the conflict between things as they are, and as they could or should be. This quest for Paradise, located as it is in the saloons of peace and hope, is a search for connection, a place to meet not only one another, but also to discover reality among the illusions, the truth amid the pipe dreams. They are seeking clear perception, and if they do not themselves arrive at this insight, we as viewers of them and with them, perceive through their eyes the ways of truth and the orders of actuality.

PART III

IMAGES OF BECOMING:
The Experience of Purgatorio

I said to my soul, be still, and wait without hope
For hope would be hope for the wrong thing; wait
   without love
For love would be love of the wrong thing; there is yet
   faith
But the faith and the love and the hope are all in the
   waiting.
Wait without thought, for you are not ready for thought:
So the darkness shall be the light, and the stillness the
   dancing.

—T. S. Eliot, "East Coker," *Four Quartets*

SIX

THE DRAMA OF PERFORMING:
The Locus of Beckett's Theatre

ESTRAGON: *Do you think God sees me?*
VLADIMIR: *You must close your eyes.*

Samuel Beckett's dramatic world begins and ends within the confines of the stage itself, for the elements of drama shape both the thematic motifs and technique of his plays. Indeed, Ruby Cohn asserts that just as "most of Beckett's fiction focuses on a man writing, so his drama focuses on a man acting."[1] Even Beckett's titles indicate the self-conscious concern with dramatic elements: the action and non-action of *Waiting for Godot*, the impossibility of a denouement in *Endgame*, the running monologue of *Krapp's Last Tape*, the buried setting and frozen time of *Happy Days*, the stark miming of the two *Acts Without Words*, and the blunt simplicity of the more recent titles: *Come and Go*, *Film*, and simply *Play*. Beckett's notes to a 1967 production of *Endgame*—"*Endgame* is only play. Nothing less"—specify the locus of his theatre: drama as performance. And when Clov requests Hamm to "stop playing," Hamm's response, "Never!" provides us with the playing time of Beckett's theatre: eternity.

In much the same way that the contemporary painter has made line and color rather than the representation of objects

---

[1]Ruby Cohn, *Currents in Contemporary Drama* (Bloomington: Indiana University Press, 1969), p. 33. Professor Cohn's writings, including her editing of the special issue of *Modern Drama* on Beckett (December, 1966), reveal her continued awareness of Beckett's use of the metaphors of theatre. For a fuller discussion of the metaphor of theatre as theatre, see Lionel Abel, *Metatheatre* (New York: Hill and Wang, 1963).

the form and content of art, Beckett's plays rely on the basic elements of theatre themselves in order to search out the root of drama, *dran:* to do, to perform. The stage as a self-contained microcosm, the search for an author-director and a script, the inability to know which role to play, and particularly the desperate need for an audience—out of these building blocks of drama Beckett has constructed his plays. The result, as Kenneth Rexroth remarked in his review of *Waiting for Godot,* is that Beckett's theatre can be perceived as "the distillation of dramatic essence."[2]

The question which has always been present in the dramatic tradition is therefore raised with intense poignancy to both Beckett's characters and to us as spectator-participants: Of what drama, if any, is one a part? More particularly, both to Beckett's characters and to us, various dilemmas are presented with dramatic immediacy. If the stage is the world, is there an author-director of the action? What is the script, or, in other terms, how free a role does a character play? And, finally, who, if anyone, responds to and evaluates the character's performance? An exploration of these dramatic elements in Beckett's plays should not only set forth a modern artist's conception of the stage as world, but also reveal the significance of that metaphor for us as participants in the drama of time and eternity.

—*I*—

THE STAGE

VLADIMIR: (looking around) *You recognize the place?*

The first scenic words of *Endgame* are: *"Bare interior."* *Act Without Words I* opens with: *"Desert. Blazing light."* *Happy Days* echoes such a setting: *"Expanse of scorched grass . . . Blazing light."* Krapp's *"table and immediately adjacent area* [are] *in strong white light. Rest of stage in darkness."* In *Play,* each character's speech is provoked by a spotlight projected on

---

[2]Kenneth Rexroth, *Bird in the Bush* (New York: New Directions, 1959), p. 82.

him. And the setting of *Waiting for Godot:* "*A country road. A tree. Evening*" has become the archetype of the barren environments of many absurdist dramas.

Beckett's characters are therefore exposed not only to each other but also to the vastness of empty space. His stage's dazzling light, instead of possessing the metaphorical connotations of insight and knowledge, has been transformed into the searching spotlight of an omniscient eye which makes men vulnerable before it. Mrs. Rooney in *All That Fall* sings: ". . . the encircling gloo-oom . . . tum tum me on," but no kindly light leads her on.

Such images of hollow men wandering in a wasteland are perhaps even more potently expressed in Beckett's distinctive images of immobility: Nell and Nagg in their ash cans, the characters of *Play* within their three grey urns, and most of all, Winnie in her mound of earth. In Act I, she is embedded above her waist; by Act II, she is buried up to her neck. Tom Driver's impatience concerning the characters of *Happy Days* is understandable: "They are planted like vegetables in the earth. They move not, neither do they sprout."[3] Pozzo's assertion in *Godot* has come true: "That's how it is on this bitch of an earth."

Whether the space Beckett's characters occupy is one of complete emptiness or of overwhelming heaviness, each, as Vladimir comments, "remains in the dark." "There's no lack of void," Estragon asserts. They are uncertain, both of their location and purpose, and this ignorance becomes the source of endless speculation. Now and then, someone may insist that he knows where he is, as Hamm states, ". . . here we're down in a hole," or as Estragon bursts forth, "I'm in hell," but the prevalent mood is incessant theorizing about each one's place in the world.

The spectator-participant of Beckett's dramas asks, as Pozzo does, "Where are we?" And our answer is Vladimir's: "I couldn't tell you." But Pozzo in his blindness rejoins: "It isn't by any chance the place known as the Board?"

---

[3]Tom F. Driver, "Unsweet Song," *Christian Century*, LXXVIII (October 11, 1961), 1209.

Beckett therefore does make it clear that one of the loci of his theatre is the stage itself. As in many of Pirandello's plays, the only reality for the characters is within the confines of the boxed stage.[4] When Estragon attempts to run offstage, Vladimir shouts: "Imbecile! There's no way out there." Earlier, when Estragon points to a lavatory in the wings, "End of the corridor, on the left," Vladimir asks; "Keep my seat." Even the long day "is very near the end of its repertory."

The particular areas in which these clown-tramps perform is that of the music-hall and circus:

VLADIMIR: *Charming evening we're having.*
ESTRAGON: *Unforgettable.*
VLADIMIR: *And it's not over.*
ESTRAGON: *Apparently not.*
VLADIMIR: *It's only beginning.*
ESTRAGON: *It's awful.*
VLADIMIR: *Worse than the pantomime.*
ESTRAGON: *The circus.*
VLADIMIR: *The music-hall.*
ESTRAGON: *The circus.*

The French playwright Anouilh originally reviewed the play as "the music-hall sketch of Pascal's *Pensee's* as played by the Fratellini clowns,"[5] but perhaps even more accurate is Professor Cohn's description of the action as "a music-hall sketch of Cartesian man performed by Chaplinesque clowns."[6] The clowns have clearly not learned their parts, for they repeatedly discuss what to do next. They are, according to Hugh Kenner, "helping the management fulfill, in a minimal way, its contract with the ticket holders."[7]

---

[4]Beckett has said that *Waiting for Godot* "does not lend itself to staging in the round—'it needs a very closed box. . . .'" Cited in Alec Reid, *All I can Manage, More Than I Could: An Approach to the Plays of Samuel Beckett* (Chester Springs, Pennsylvania: Dufour Editions, 1968), p. 19.

[5]*Arts* #400, January 27, 1953.

[6]Cohn, *Samuel Beckett: The Comic Gamut* (New Brunswick: Rutgers University Press, 1962), p. 211.

[7]Hugh Kenner, *Samuel Beckett: A Critical Study* (Berkeley: University of California Press, 1968), p. 135.

Endgame suggests even more the characters' self-consciousness that their world is a stage. When Clov insists that he will leave Hamm, and adds, "What is there to keep me here?" Hamm exclaims: "The dialogue." Later, Hamm angrily informs Clov that he is speaking "an aside, ape. Did you never hear an aside before?" and, after a pause, adds: "I'm warming up for my last soliloquy." Hamm responds to Clov's discovery of a small boy within the telescope's sight with the words: "Not an underplot, I trust." When Clov finally decides to leave, he explains: "This is what we call making an exit." And in the closing moments of the play, Hamm performs his own farewell by discarding his whistle and his dog and by again covering his face with the bloody handerchief. The grandeur of man the actor, John Sheedy has perceptively noted, "has shrunk to a single possibility: the ham actor."[8]

Such self-reflections on the theatre as theatre imply not only that the characters are imprisoned on the stage, but also that they are required both to improvise the script and to play interchanging roles of actors and directors.

— II —

THE ACTOR-DIRECTOR AND HIS SCRIPT

VLADIMIR: *Will you not play?*
ESTRAGON: *Play at what?*

All four characters in *Waiting for Godot* are performers: Lucky and Pozzo do solo numbers; Vladimir and Estragon engage in duets, including playing the roles of Lucky and Pozzo. Lucky is forced to play the fool; he must move and dance and think at the crack of Pozzo's whip. When Lucky finally does speak, his lengthy tirade-lament is intolerable for his audience both onstage and off. Pozzo himself wants the attention of all. Ostentatiously spraying his throat, spitting, and then clearing his throat, he demands: "Is everybody listening? Is everybody

---

[8]John J. Sheedy, "The Comic Apocalypse of King Hamm," *Modern Drama*, IX (December, 1966), 315.

ready? . . . I don't like talking in a vacuum." Pozzo insists on being the center of his controlled audience: "But be a little more attentive, for pity's sake, otherwise we'll never get anywhere." And after all his bombast, he is still begging for a complimentary response: "How did you find me? Good? Fair? Middling? Poor? Positively bad? . . . I have such need of encouragement!" Pozzo's role is one of power, and he finds it difficult to reconcile his human weakness and his theatrical strength.

All of the characters must improvise roles and invent a script, and therefore they try various poses for fit, just as they do their shoes and bowlers. They play psychoanalyst and confessional priest for one another, acrobat, tyrant, menial, long lost friend, and aggrieved lover as well as many other roles. They try everything at random; given a blank piece of time, they are forced to extemporize. The only action Lucky and Pozzo cannot perform is to stay; they must always be on the move. And the only script Vladimir and Estragon cannot change is to go; they must continue to wait for Godot. These two givens are certainly mandates about which, as the play insists in its opening lines, "Nothing [is] to be done." Since the playing time provided for them is indeterminate, each day they must, according to Judith Radke, " 'play out' another act in the unnumbered succession of performances in their life-long drama."[9]

The characters in *Endgame* are also aware of their theatrical roles. "Nicely put, that," comments Hamm after one of his flourishes. He, as an anti-heroic version of Hamlet and a decrepit image of Prospero ("Our revels now are ended"), directs a play within a play: the endgame with its chess-like moves and its antagonist as Death itself.[10] From his wheelchair as throne, he oversees the performances of Nell and

[9]Judith J. Radke, "The Theatre of Samuel Beckett: 'Une durée à animer,'" *Yale French Studies* 29 (Spring-Summer, 1962), 64.

[10]Jan Kott speaks of fate's game with Oedipus, Lear, and Hamm/Clov as a game of chess with an electric computer which, as it learns to anticipate each move, must win in the end, "King Lear or Endgame" in *Shakespeare Our Contemporary*, trans. Boleslaw Taborski (New York: Doubleday, 1964), pp. 87–124.

Nagg, who tell stories reminiscent of an April afternoon on Lake Como. At the end of the drama, as Hamm throws his whistle toward the audience, he comments: "With my compliments." He is now ready to assume the motionless pose with which he began: He theatrically covers his face with the bloody handerchief and reflects on his own past, present, and future performance: "Since that's the way we're playing it . . . let's play it that way . . . and speak no more about it . . . speak no more" [all ellipses in text].

In *Krapp's Last Tape*, the roles of director, performer, and audience are all inextricably tied together. A self-proclaimed author, Krapp directs his recreation of the past both by listening to the old tapes and by performing for his last tape. Professor Cohn perceptively observes:

> Krapp is an active audience for his own tape, reacting explosively to the role that he played in the past; in past tapes, Krapp was already an active audience, reacting to old roles. And we imagine another Krapp who will react as we do to the tape-role that Krapp records on stage.[11]

Beckett's own statement in his writings on Proust comes dramatically alive in *Krapp's Last Tape*: "Life is a succession of habits, since the individual is a succession of individuals; the world being a projection of the individual's consciousness. . . ."[12] The tapes preserve Krapp's many lost selves and speak to him and for him much as "all the dead voices" whisper and rustle in *Waiting for Godot*. Sandra Gilbert has commented that *Krapp's Last Tape* is "ultimately no more than a machine (literally so in this case) through which the consciousness—the soul, even—of a man is projected onto a stage in the presence of an audience."[13] What we therefore experience is a man improvising his own script and therefore inventing his own reality.

Performing songs and reciting prayers and fragments of poetry, Winnie waits for the bell that will end another of her

---

[11]Cohn, *Currents in Contemporary Drama*, p. 229.

[12]Samuel Beckett, *Proust* (London: Chatto and Windus, 1931), p. 8.

[13]Sandra M. Gilbert, "All the Dead Voices," *Drama Survey*, VI (Spring, 1968), 257.

Happy Days. She preens herself by filing her nails, combing her hair, brushing her teeth, and applying lipstick as if she were getting ready to make an entrance. When Willie finally crawls over the mound at the end of the play, dressed in the costume of formal attire, he too appears ready to assume a new role. Both Winnie and Willie are actor and audience, for each needs the other to confirm his own reality.

Beckett's characters attempt to create a reality, to fulfill a role, and to invent a pose which will carry them through to the end, through the interminable waiting. What sustains them in their performance, and this is one of Beckett's unique contributions to our post-Pirandellian theatre, is the presence of another. If they are given an audience, they seem somehow able to endure the waiting.

— III —

THE AUDIENCE

VLADIMIR: ·*At me too someone is looking, of me too someone is saying, He is sleeping, he knows nothing, let him sleep on.*

In each of Beckett's plays, the characters desperately want an audience, someone who listens to them, someone who looks at them, someone who recognizes them. Vladimir's second and briefer exchange with the messenger from Godot opens with the tramp's question: "Do you not recognize me?" and closes with Vladimir's hesitant and then violent insistence on being seen:

> *Tell him . . .* (he hesitates) . . . *tell him you saw me and that . . .* (he hesitates) . . . *that you saw me.* (Pause. Vladimir advances, the Boy recoils. Vladimir halts, the Boy halts. With sudden violence.) *You're sure you saw me, you won't come and tell me to-morrow that you never saw me!* (Silence.)

Just before the boy arrived, Vladimir tells Estragon: "It seemed to me he [Pozzo] saw us." But Pozzo, as Estragon reminds his fellow-clown, is blind.

Yet it was Estragon who earlier in Act II raised the question: "Do you think God sees me?" Vladimir's answer, "You must close your eyes," epitomizes Beckett's complex imagery: the attitude of believing prayer, the appearance of sleep leading to death, the stance of attempting to engage in memory and fantasy, and the childlike notion that if one closes his own eyes, he is invisible to the other. But when Estragon then does close his eyes as he is doing "the tree," he "staggers worse," for he is now blind.[14] Brandishing his fists, Estragon shouts a kyrie: "God have pity on me!" Vladimir, "vexed," responds: "And me?" Estragon persists: "On me! On me! Pity! On me!" The stage directions then read: *"Enter Pozzo and Lucky Pozzo is blind."*

This entire scene, in both its language and action, therefore prompts the reader-spectator to raise Estragon's question: "Are you sure it [Pozzo] wasn't him [Godot]?" And Vladimir's response is exactly mine: "Not at all! (*Less sure.*) Not at all! (*Still less sure.*) Not at all!" Beckett, never limiting his characters, symbols, and imagery to one interpretation, nevertheless in this play hovers about the possible relationship of Pozzo to Godot and of Godot to God and focuses our attention on the eyes of all three.[15]

[14]Alan Schneider, the first American director of *Waiting for Godot*, in an interview, stated:

> I wrote to him [Beckett] about Godot and said I couldn't understand about this 'Let's do the tree for fun' business while they're doing exercises, and in almost every production the actor playing Estragon simply stands on one leg and holds his arms out like the branches of a tree. He wrote back and said that's exercise fifty-two in the yogi series of exercises, and he drew me a little diagram—the 'tree' is propped up, and with the arms in the position of prayer (a balancing exercise). The next line is 'Do you think God is watching me?' If he is accidentally in a position of prayer, then becomes aware of the position into which he has strayed, and wonders whether, by accident, that position of prayer has had some impact on God, then that transition becomes a logical and organic thing. To Beckett it was crystal clear.

"Reality Is Not Enough," *Tulane Drama Review*, IX (Spring, 1965), 138–139.

[15]V. A. Kolve has developed the notion that Pozzo's role is possibly a caricature of a tyrannical, vengeful, and unchanging Old Testament Jehovah, "Religious Language in *Waiting for Godot*," *Centennial Review*, XI (Winter, 1967), 102–127.

Tradition has given us rich imagery concerning the relationship of eyes and the perception of truth. The blind poet-
prophets (Homer, Tiresias, Samson) have true insight:
"Perhaps he can see into the future," concludes Estragon
about Pozzo. To lose one's eyesight (Oedipus, Gloucester, and
again Samson) often implies that one has arrived at inner
perception. Although commentators invariably stress Pozzo's
weakened condition in Act II, his tyrannical power has also
disappeared. He now realizes that he himself lives without
being able to control time, as he did in Act I: "The blind have
no notion of time. The things of time are hidden from them
too."Even Pozzo's last words center on light and darkness:
"They give birth astride of a grave, then it's night once more."
Birth comes in the presence of death, light appears but a
moment, and again it is dark. Literal blindness may be the
price of spiritual perception, just as death is the prerequisite
for rebirth within the tragic experience.

Vladimir and Estragon's desire to have Godot come is an
attempt to experience a recognition scene, to arrive at self-
discovery. But ambivalence dominates. To be seen by God, to
be in his presence, is to be blinded, if not to die, for as God
said to Moses: ". . . man shall not see me and live" (Exodus
33:20). If Godot comes, "we'll be saved," but an awareness
pervades their thinking that his coming may possibly destroy
them. The waited-for one may be a merciful savior or he may
be a vengeful judge of their performance. There is an even
chance if one is in the immediate presence of deity: one of the
thieves was saved, and the other was damned. Meanwhile
Vladimir and Estragon wait, caught in the tension between
blind faith and blind fate.

Blind Hamm in *Endgame* prophesies to Clov: "One day
you'll be blind, like me. You'll be sitting there, a speck in the
void, in the dark, for ever, like me." Perhaps that "one day"
will be the day Clov sees Hamm's eyes:

> HAMM: *Did you ever see my eyes?*
> CLOV: *No.*
> HAMM: *Did you never have the curiosity, while I was sleeping,
> to take off my glasses and look at my eyes?*

CLOV: *Pulling back the lids?* (Pause.) *No.*
HAMM: *One of these days I'll show them to you.*

Hamm needs Clov to act for him and to be his audience, for he gives continual orders to Clov. Not one of Hamm's instructions is more specific than that he be located in the exact center of the room. Hamm not only wants to be director of the *theatrum mundi*, but he also needs the reassurance that his position is *axis mundi*. Hamm desires even the complete attention and obedience of Clov's toy black dog:

HAMM: *Is he gazing at me?*
CLOV: *Yes.*
HAMM: *As if he were asking me to take him for a walk?*
CLOV: *If you like.*
HAMM: *Or as if he were begging me for a bone. Leave him like that, standing there imploring me.*

Hamm's dictatorial commands to direct the action are transformed into a plea to be looked at, to be listened to, to have another as audience. To be seen may be the prerequisite to arriving at the ability to see.

Krapp's wish is to be heard. He replays his tapes, but since no one else hears his own words, the result is narcissistic, even masturbatory. As the play ends with Krapp sitting motionless and the tape running on in silence, there is nothing left to say, for no one has listened.

Winnie is already in the exact center of the mound, but her great fear is that before the bell rings, she will be deprived of a response. She needs to talk, but still more she needs a listener:

Ah, yes, if only I could bear to be alone, I mean prattle away with not a soul to hear. (Pause.) Not that I flatter myself you hear much, no Willie, God forbid. (Pause.) Days perhaps when you hear nothing. (Pause.) But days too when you answer. (Pause.) So that I may say at all times, even when you do not answer and perhaps hear nothing, something of this is being heard, I am not merely talking to myself, that is in the wilderness, a thing I could never bear to do—for any length of time.

As Nathan Scott comments, speech, for Winnie, is "a way of creating a kind of camp-fire, about which one can huddle by way of staving off the surrounding wilderness."[16] And the wilderness, the barrenness, is also within: "I say I used to think that I would learn to talk alone. (*Pause.*) By that I mean to myself, the wilderness."

Winnie's obsessive attention to her spectacles, her mirror, and her telescope reveals her awareness of the importance of looking and seeing. She frequently closes her eyes in order to engage in fantasy and pleasant memories, and most of all, to help the time pass. Her meditations include a reference to the Scripture passage: "Where two or three are gathered in my name, there am I in the midst of them" (Matthew 18:20):

> *Can you see me from there I wonder, I still wonder.* (Pause.) *No?* (Back front.) *Oh I know it does not follow when two are gathered together*—(faltering)—*in this way*—(normal)—*that because one sees the other the other sees the one, life has taught me that . . . too.*

Yet, throughout Act I, Winnie has the "strange feeling that someone is looking at [her]" and she adds at the opening of Act II:

> *Someone is looking at me still.* (Pause.) *Caring for me still.* (Pause.) *That is what I find so wonderful.* (Pause.) *Eyes on my eyes.*

When Willie finally appears, Winnie suggests: "That's right, Willie, look at me. (*Pause.*) Feast your old eyes, Willie." But a few minutes later, she changes her attitude: "Don't look at me like that!" Yet at the end of the play, "*they look at each other.*" She is not alone in the wilderness; another has recognized her. The two have sung the same tune, they have laughed at the same joke, and now they have looked at each other. Professor Cohn asks rhetorically: "What more can love do, on the happiest day?"[17]

In Beckett's most recent works, the plaint for recogni-

---

[16]Nathan A. Scott, Jr., *Samuel Beckett* (London: Bowes and Bowes, 1965), p. 122.

[17]Cohn, *Samuel Beckett: The Comic Gamut*, p. 259.

tion is intensified. The pathetic queries of the Second Woman in *Play* are addressed to a world in which no one seems to love or to care: "Are you listening to me? Is anyone listening to me? Is anyone looking at me? Is anyone bothering about me at all?"

Film, Beckett's short movie in which Buster Keaton played his last major role, presents a protagonist who, the manuscript indicates, "is sundered into object (O) and Eye (E), the former in flight, the latter in pursuit." He therefore intends to remove all perception—human perception, animal perception, and divine perception; he tears into pieces a print of "the face of God the Father, the eyes staring at him severely." He becomes so obsessed with eyes that he sees them peering at him from every object. By removing all perception of himself, he thinks that he will cease to exist, that he will have committed suicide. But he is not allowed this escape, for at the end, we are presented with the image of the man sitting bowed, his head in his hands. He cannot avoid the presence of his own ego, his own self-perception. The manuscript itself indicates in the film's opening: "Search of non-being in flight from extraneous perception breaking down in inescapability of self-perception." He, whether he wishes to be or not, is audience to himself.

—IV—

THE HUMAN DRAMA

POZZO: *Who are you?*
VLADIMIR: *We are men.*

One of the fundamental needs of modern man is to be liberated from the bondage of his own subjectivity and to find a place of detachment adequate to arrive at some objectivity. This is certainly one of the major rationales for Beckett's characters in their craving for an audience. Vladimir and Estragon each want the other to enter his pains, troubles, and dreams. "All the dead voices" want to "talk about their lives," for "to have lived is not enough for them, they have to talk about it." They need one another as a confirmation of their own reality; they must, as Estragon suggests, "always find something, eh Didi, to give us the impression we exist?" They do not belong ("We're not from these parts, Sir," says Estragon to Pozzo), and thus they desperately want to attain certainty about their location and purpose both from each other and from everyone else who comes along. Estragon is "pale for weariness," he says, because of his action "of climbing heaven and gazing on the likes of us." Such self-transcendence may be an attempt to gain the vision of Jacob's ladder: "Surely the Lord is in this place; and I knew it not" (Genesis 28:16).[18] For the two tramps, Godot is not only the one waited-for, but he is also the one who will be an audience for them. They hope that he will give recognition and provide relationship. The impersonal and indifferent gaze of the universe will be transformed into a situation in which another may listen to them and see them. Instead of the classical tragic protagonist who attempts to play the role of God, Beckett's characters tragicomically want to have Godot as audience.

But actually to be observed, to be recognized, to be seen, as Eva Metman suggests, by "a knowing witness,"[19] Beckett's characters know they cannot endure. They are vaguely aware, as Hamlet was much more so, that if they faced their specific situations without the masks of grotesque jest and mad farce, they would destroy themselves. So too in *Endgame*, when Nell asks Nagg if he can see her, he answers, "Hardly," and Nell replies, "So much the better, so much the better." An absolutely clear vision of their predicament would only result in self-destructive pity and madness. "Imagine," states Hamm,

---

[18]The passage may also allude to Shelley's poem, "To the Moon":

Art thou pale for weariness
Of climbing heaven and gazing on the earth,
    Wandering companionless
Among the stars that have a different birth. . . .

[19]Eva Metman, "Reflections on Samuel Beckett's Plays," in *Samuel Beckett*, ed. Martin Esslin (Englewood Cliffs: Prentice-Hall, 1965), p. 128. Professor Metman also calls attention to Nietzsche's statement in *Thus Spake Zarathustra*: "The God that saw all, *even man*—that God could not but die! Man could not endure that such a witness should live."

"if a rational being came back to earth, wouldn't he be liable to get ideas in his head if he observed us long enough." But no being, rational or otherwise, has yet come to observe the performances of Beckett's characters.

Therefore, in the interim, the time of waiting, each must provide an audience for the other. It is thus not unimportant that all of Beckett's major plays contain complementary pairs of characters. The relationships of Gogo and Didi, Lucky and Pozzo, Hamm and Clov, Nagg and Nell, Winnie and Willie, and even Krapp and his tape-recorder move through phases of masochism, scorn, charity, parasitism, and faithfulness. Master and servant, executioner and victim, lover and loved— each one of the pair assumes all these and many other roles. Each wants to be independent but dreads being parted. Each frequently pretends to get on famously alone, but knows he is destined to remain with the other. But each is given another, if it is only his earlier or other self, as an audience. For in Beckett's world, men are tied to one another:

ESTRAGON: *We're not tied?*
VLADIMIR: *I don't hear a word you're saying.*
ESTRAGON: *I'm asking if we're tied.*
VLADIMIR: *Tied?*
ESTRAGON: *Tied.*
VLADIMIR: *How do you mean tied?*
ESTRAGON: *Down.*
VLADIMIR: *But to whom?*
ESTRAGON: *To your man.*
VLADIMIR: *To Godot? Tied to Godot? What an idea! No question of it.* (Pause.) *For the moment.*

A moment later, Lucky enters, tied "*by means of a rope passed round his neck*" to Pozzo, who commands, rope-end in one hand, whip in the other. Rosette Lamont suggests that the rope is reminiscent of "an unsevered umbilical cord," and adds that "two separate beings have joined symbiotically: the result a monstrous, indivisible mass of humanity."[20] The relationship of Lucky and Pozzo is one of bondage, of imprisonment.

---

[20]Rosette Lamont, "Beckett's Metaphysics of Choiceless Awareness," in *Samuel Beckett Now,* ed. Melvin J. Friedman (Chicago: University of Chicago Press, 1970), p. 211.

But Vladimir and Estragon also have a rope in common: the rope which Estragon, who always forgets, will bring tomorrow so that they can commit suicide by hanging themselves from the tree. This bond of life and death unites them.

The two tramps and all of the other characters on Beckett's stage are, as men always are, exceedingly ambivalent about the fact of being tied to Godot and to one another. If Vladimir and Estragon believe they are tied to Godot in the bondage of puppet-like strings, they know that they have lost their freedom. But if, as contemporary man more frequently experiences, they have lost all relationship to the transcendent and have also become alienated from all human bonds, they are placed in dreadful freedom. Their dominant problem, as J. R. Moore states, is

> to be detached or not to be detached. Complete detachment is solipsistic insanity. Complete engagement would also be madness, like holding the palm of your hand over the flame from a gas burner.[21]

Between such tensions, all of Beckett's actors balance. Between freedom and dread, they hesitate; they can only wait. In the interim, they perform scenes and enact roles.

But the play of which they are a part is not a drama of action in which the characters must engage in a quest of discovery. Rather, they are aware that they are participants in a drama of passion. And to be part of a drama of passion implies several dimensions for Beckett's theatre.[22]

Clearly, each of the characters suffers both physical and spiritual anguish. Hamm continues to ask: "Is it not time for

---

[21]J. R. Moore, "Some Night Thoughts of Beckett," *Massachusetts Review*, VIII (Summer, 1967), 537.

[22]Several critics have discussed the parallels between Beckett's characters and the passion of Jesus Christ. For *Endgame*, cf. Sheedy, above, pp. 310–318, and Cohn, *Samuel Beckett: The Comic Gamut*, pp. 226–242. For *Waiting for Godot*, cf. Kay Baxter, *Speak What We Feel* (London: SCM Press, 1964), pp. 9–19, and William R. Mueller and Josephine Jacobsen, "Samuel Beckett's Long Saturday: To Wait or Not to Wait?" in *Man in the Modern Theatre*, ed. Nathan A. Scott, Jr. (Richmond: John Knox Press, 1965), pp. 76–97.

my pain-killer?" "When for a moment," Beckett writes of Proust, "the boredom of living is replaced by the suffering of being," the individual enters the perilous zones which not only are "dangerous, precarious, and painful," but also are "mysterious and fertile."[23] Suffering, even on Beckett's stage, may lead to insight.

Besides suffering, a drama of passion also implies a state of being acted upon. Some of the characters tyrannize others: Pozzo uses his whip on Lucky; Hamm controls every movement of Clov. The whistle in *Act Without Words I*, an external force which man can neither control nor please, finally compels the protagonist simply to look at his hands. All such gestures lead to the awareness that no human action is wholly self-determined.

Beckett's characters must therefore cultivate suffering patience, for the imprisoned I cannot be liberated in Beckett's theatre by some sort of self-generated exercise. No particular action, no performing role, will provide the magical escape from their predicament.

On their confined stages, Beckett's characters therefore gradually realize the meaningful nuances of the opening line of his first major play: "Nothing to be done." In the haunting images of silence and motionlessness at the end of each of his plays, one sees the central drama of Beckett's theatre. For in these dramas of performing, the fundamental unwritten stage direction is: Be still.

[23]Beckett, *Proust*, p. 8.

§ SEVEN §

THE PROCESS OF DYING:
The Plays of Edward Albee

In Edward Albee's play of 1967, *Everything in the Garden*, one
of the major characters comments:

> You should have been in London in the war. You would have
> learned about death... and violence.... All those nights in the
> shelters, with the death going on. Death and dying. Always take the
> former if you can.

Albee has not been following this advice, for his plays, culminating in his play of 1971, *All Over*, have centered largely
on the process of dying.

The settings, characters, and actions of his plays are
haunted by death, both natural and violent. Indeed, as Ruby
Cohn has commented, "the shadow of death darkens all Albee's plays."[1] In the presence of "the death going on," the real
self is made visible, for illusions are unmasked at this moment.
Human freedom may become aware of its limitations, and
therefore self-knowledge may be achieved. Those who confront death in Albee's plays sometimes experience an encounter with terror but more frequently they experience an
arrival at rest and peace. And the process itself for both participant and spectator is a cleansing, a cathartic purging.

---

[1]Ruby Cohn, *Edward Albee*, University of Minnesota Pamphlets on
American Writers, No. 77 (Minneapolis: University of Minnesota Press,
1969), p. 44.

— I —

"Is he dead?" asks the wife as *All Over* begins. We are in the presence of death, but we never see the dying husband who is behind the hospital screen. Therefore we must concentrate on those who have come to wait out the ritual of his dying: his wife, his mistress, his son and daughter, his best friend, a doctor, and a nurse. The New York production with its cold spotlights and brilliant metallic furniture accurately conveyed the atmosphere of a high black vault, for both the characters on stage and the audience are participating in a deathwatch.

But the various characters, just as we in the audience, view the ritual of the deathwatch in different ways. The Best Friend relies on tradition:

> *It is more or less required that you be . . . I think: here. Family. Isn't it one of our customs? that if a man has not outlived his wife and children—will not outlive them . . . they gather?*

The daughter in her cynicism comments that the mass media has brought out a small crowd: "the kind of crowd you'd get for a horse with sunstroke, if it were summer. . . . They're lounging, nothing better to do, and if it weren't night and a weekend, I doubt they'd linger." In reply, the Nurse focuses, as the entire play does, on the process of dying: "That's the final test of fame, isn't it, the degree of it: which is newsworthy, the act of dying itself, or merely the death." With the Kennedys and with King, she continues, the public was cheated, and possessed a kind of anger at having missed the dying. Only in Pope John's dying could one "share," for in those "two weeks of the vilest agony," the confrontation with death became a meaningful experience for the public. In the encounter with death within this play, the Mistress and particularly the Wife become more aware of their own limitations. The Mistress asks tentatively at the beginning of the play, "This is . . . ritual, is it not?" and later asserts: "You can't suffer with a man because he's dead; his dying, yes. The only horror in participating is . . . well, another time." The suffering horror is revealed in the Wife's confession at the end: "All we've done . . . is think about ourselves." She realizes that she is unwilling to sacrifice:

> *Selfless love? I don't think so; we love to be loved, and when it's taken away . . . then why not rage . . . or pule. All we've done is think about ourselves. Ultimately.*

Each of the characters is dead to every other; the failure of love is a form of dying, as Albee declared in a *New York Times* interview: "I write plays about how people waste their lives. The people in this play [*All Over*] have not *lived* their lives; that's what they're screaming and crying about."[2] Indeed, the expected last line of the play, "All over," encapsulates the drama: the husband has died, the news of his passing will be broadcast all over, and most of all, for the characters and the audience the ritual of participation in dying has concluded.

—II—

Albee's plays have frequently concentrated their action in a ritual of a deathwatch with a priest, actual or incognito, as officiant. In *All Over,* the Doctor rather self-consciously comments: "I'm rather like a priest: you have me for the limits, for birth and dying, *and* for the minor cuts and scratches in between."

The earlier play, *The Sandbox,* in its brief action portrays an embryonic and more satirical version of *All Over*. The sandbox is Grandma's grave, Mommy and Daddy hire a musician to contribute to the rite, and the Young Man in his calisthenics and in his comforting words to dying Grandma assumes the role of a benediction-giving priest. Grandma is vivacious even while dying, but the inauthentic existence of Mommy and Daddy has not been touched at all. They have been playing funeral; they have not actually participated in the ritualistic process of dying. Only spectators, they leave with the same indifference and blindness with which they arrived.

[2]*The New York Times,* April 18, 1971.

After Jack's murder by his friends in *Everything in the Garden*, Albee's stage directions indicate, "*This is a wake and the ladies have sorrow on their faces.*" Only Jenny is disturbed by the cold-blooded murder which was committed to keep the truth quiet; the others remain detached. By the end of the drama, Jenny too is objectively insisting that the garden in which Jack has been buried should be "well planted and taken care of; kept up. I think it should look like all the others. Don't you think so?" The corruption of values has made their existence a living lie.

In two of Albee's plays, *Who's Afraid of Virginia Woolf?* and *Tiny Alice*, a character playing the role of a priest is central to the core of the drama. George's intonation of a Requiem Mass indicates a ritualistic burial of the illusory son. The sacrifice of the child as a scapegoat ("the poor lamb," says Martha) to exorcise the evil spirit of illusion is the last game George initiates: "We're going to play this one to the death." Martha at first refuses to participate in the burial ritual; however, she engages in a confession simultaneous with George's Latin phrases: "I have tried, oh God I have tried. . . ." Nick and Honey are primarily passive spectators to this event, but later Honey does come forth with a Latin response to George's litany, and Nick comments: "Jesus Christ, I think I understand this." Out of this process of dying, purgation and purification emerge. The sacrificial death of the son brings atonement and reconciliation at dawn on a Sunday morning.

Julian in *Tiny Alice* is actually a lay brother, but he had always wanted to be a priest, and within the drama, he performs the roles of both officiant and sacrifice. Albee suggested to John Gielgud, who played the title role in the New York production, that Julian is "the innocent coming into this rather extraordinary assemblage of people."[3] He would have become a priest, but he could not reconcile his idea of God with the god men create in their own image. The Butler accurately tells Julian: "You are of the cloth but have not taken it"; Julian is not yet ready to die to the world. His

---

[3]"John Gielgud and Edward Albee Talk about the Theater," *The Atlantic Monthly* (April 1965), p. 68.

religious struggle is now put to the test when he is brought to the castle of Miss Alice.[4] His "special priesthood," as his cardinal pointed out to him, is with Alice, the unseen abstract being, and he is to be sacrificed to her. Although he had always hungered for such a vocation ("I have . . . dreamed of sacrifice," and later, "oh, martyrdom, to be that. To be able . . . to be that"), he cannot accept it when it is offered to him. He is torn, as Albee explained in his speech at the Billy Rose Theatre following the opening of the play, "between the selflessness of service and the conspicuous splendor of martyrdom."[5] In his hesitation, the Lawyer mortally wounds Julian with a pistol. When all exit, the audience is left alone to participate in Julian's dying on his wedding day:

> I have never dreamed of it, never imagined what it would be like. I have—oh, yes—dwelt (Laughs at the word) . . . dwelt . . . on the fact of it, the . . . principle, but I have not imagined dying. Death . . . yes. Not being, but not the act of . . . dying?

To dream of sacrifice may be consoling, but to imagine dying is to face the possibility of nothingness. As he dies, throwing out his arms to receive Alice, his form is in the position of a crucifixion. In his final self-delusion, Julian creates and believes in what he knows does not exist. He has sacrificed himself to a god created by man in his own image. He has died for nothing.

— *III* —

To give one's life for another, the action of sacrificial love, has certainly been one of the major motifs in Albee's dramatizations of the process of dying. In *The Zoo Story*, Peter's murder of Jerry finds its source in Peter's earlier indifference and cold-

---

[4]For a discussion of *Tiny Alice* as a morality play in which Julian is tempted by the World (the Butler), the Flesh (Miss Alice), and the Devil (the Lawyer), see Mary Elizabeth Campbell, "The Tempters in Albee's *Tiny Alice*," *Modern Drama*, XIII (May, 1970), 23–33.

[5]Cited in *The Playwrights Speak*, ed. Walter Wager (New York: Dell Publishing Company, 1967), p. 34.

ness towards others. Jerry, however, has staged his own act of dying; it is an action of passion; his suicide is transformed into an act of martyrdom. At the cost of his own life, Jerry causes Peter to become aware of man's universal animality ("You're an animal, too") in order to rescue Peter's humanity. Peter is awakened from his spiritual deadness, and Jerry has arrived at the place he desired amid his restlessness: "You have comforted me. Dear Peter." Although both are, as Julian was in *Tiny Alice*, in a God-forsaken plight at the end ("Oh my God!"), both have gone "a long distance correctly"; they have arrived at a perception of what it means to face death.

But the opposite of sacrificial love has also intrigued Albee. Not to be willing to give one's self to another implies indifference and hate which leads to murder. Ironically, the murder in *Everything in the Garden* is committed by the very women who earlier were very willing to give themselves to another in prostitution. In *The Death of Bessie Smith*, the neglect of hospital employees, according to Albee's interpretation, contributed to the death of the singer. The Nurse tells Bessie's chauffeur, "YOU WAIT! You just sit down and wait!" and meanwhile, Bessie bleeds to death. All of these ordinary people are caught in their own predicaments, and the failure of love (whether the love of the Nurse for her father, the Intern, and the Orderly or the love of one's neighbor) leads to death.

The relationship of the failure of love and the terror of death is the core of *A Delicate Balance*. Harry and Edna, coming for shelter and comfort to their neighbors, Tobias and Agnes, insist that fear has overwhelmed them:

> HARRY: *It was like being lost: very young again, with the dark, and lost. There was no . . . thing . . . to be . . . frightened of, but . . .*
> EDNA: WE WERE FRIGHTENED . . . AND THERE WAS NOTHING.

The terror to be faced is the darkness of death, nothingness itself. The household of Agnes and Tobias does not respond to this plea; the inhabitants, as someone has suggested, are "Bad Samaritans." Indeed, in playful conversational interchange, which nevertheless has meaningful nuances, Claire suggests that Tobias kill his wife, Agnes recommends that Claire kill herself, and Claire later flippantly asks: "Why don't you die?" When the distraught daughter of Agnes and Tobias enters the room with a pistol, she is putting into action the deep hatred verging on murder present in the entire household. Claire's perceptivity, as usual, is accurate:

> '*Love*' *is not the problem. You love Agnes and Agnes loves Julia and Julia loves me and I love you. We all love each other. . . . Yes; to the depths of our self-pity and our greed. What else but love?*

As she cynically remarks later: "I tell ya, there are so many martyrdoms here." But no one lives or dies for another; instead the play conveys the death of marital love (the daughter's past four marriages, the disintegrating marriages of Agnes and Tobias and of Harry and Edna), the death of family love, and the death of friendship. Agnes' response to Tobias' story of the cat he had killed represents the larger action of the play: "Well, what else could you have done? There was nothing to be done; there was no . . . meeting between you." Death has conquered love in this drama.

— IV —

Not only in the relationship of neighbors, but more especially in the relationship of parents and children, Albee portrays the lack of love which leads to death. Mommy and Daddy place Grandma in the sandbox as if she were an animal. In *The American Dream*, Mommy and Daddy not only continue their cold indifference to Grandma, but they have emasculated their son. When his twin arrives as the American Dream, Grandma, who possesses the enduring and pioneer convictions of an authentic American Dream, leaves. Questioned about Grandma's leaving, Albee replied that her dying is really a departure

> from a form of life that is a great deal more dead than anything else. I guess I meant her specifically to die, but not in the sense

that we understand die; to move out of the death within life situation that everybody else in that play was in.[6]

Amid the sterility of the household with its worship of materialistic values, Grandma's authentic existence—symbolized by her omniscience—contrasts sharply with the life-lie of the rest of the family.

The death of a son and its influence on the parents' love for one another figures prominently in two of Albee's plays. In *A Delicate Balance*, Agnes comments about their son's death: "It was an unreal time: I thought Tobias was out of love with me—or, rather, was tired of it, when Teddy died, as if that had been the string." The result of this alienation between the couple is what Agnes described as "Such... silent... sad, disgusted... love."

Although as Professor Cohn has indicated, "death lies like a sediment in Martha's gin, Nick's bourbon, Honey's brandy, and mainly George's 'bergin'"[7] in *Who's Afraid of Virginia Woolf?*, the lacerating dialogue and figurative acts of murder lead to a renewal of love. As Martha recalls the time she knocked down George in a wrestling match, George's sudden appearance with a short-barreled shotgun which opens into a colorful Chinese parasol indicates his murderous intent. "You?... Kill me?... That's a laugh," comments Martha to which George replies, "Well, now, I might... some day." Later, George, while grabbing Martha's throat, shouts, "I'LL KILL YOU!" to which Martha responds, "Murderer. Mur... der... er." George's destruction of the fantasy of the son does kill part of Martha and part of himself; it has been their joint creation. Suicide, premeditated homicide, and martyrdom are all intermingled in this mercy killing. The child born of the mind for secret pleasure is killed by an act of the will for public suffering, and the birthday of his assuming manhood becomes his death day. As told by George, the cause of the son's death occurred in the identical manner in which he earlier had recounted the accident of killing his father: "He

---

[6]Cited in Michael E. Rutenberg, *Edward Albee: Playwright in Protest* (New York: Avon Books, 1969), p. 74.

[7]Cohn, p. 17.

was... killed... late in the afternoon... on a country road, with his learner's permit in his pocket, he swerved, to avoid a porcupine, and drove straight into a... large tree." George as son and as father therefore is himself dying in this act of self-sacrificial love. By symbolically eating the telegram containing the news of the son's death, George is perhaps performing a eucharistic sacramental act.[8] Later, one of Martha's stage directions reads "*a hint of communion in this,*" all of which appears to fulfill George's prophecy: "... it's going to make your performance tonight look like an Easter pageant." Out of this cauldron of suffering, the son's death leads to the resurrection of those present. The sacrifice, in the word's etymology, has once more, if only for a moment, "made holy" the relationship of marital love.

In the experience of death therefore, whether as a participant in the dying of another or in the encounter with death itself, one is attempting, as Northrop Frye suggests, "to recapture a lost rapport with the natural cycle."[9] One could add that the experience of death in Albee's plays also attempts to recapture a lost rapport with other men, both family and neighbors, intimates and strangers.

—V—

Existential philosophy has reminded us that in the encounter with death, man faces the mystery of Being and Nothingness. Death brings man to the threshold of authentic existence; death is all over, universal as well as conclusive. In such a spirit, Tolstoy in his old age could say to Gorky: "If a man has learned to think, no matter what he may think about, he is

[8]For an interpretation of *Who's Afraid of Virginia Woolf?* which develops the play's mythic relationships to Easter, see Rictor Norton, "Folklore and Myth in *Who's Afraid of Virginia Woolf?*" *Renascence*, 23 (1971), 159–167.
[9]Northrop Frye, *Fables of Identity: Studies in Poetic Mythology* (New York: Harcourt, Brace and World, 1963), p. 15.

always thinking of his own death."[10] So too Albee at age forty-three could say in a *New York Times* interview:

> I had an awareness of death when I was 15, but I turned 36 or 37 before I became aware that *I*, Edward Albee, was going to die. The realization did not fill me with dread. I simply became aware of the fact that this is the only time around for me.[11]

These two quotations play counterpoint to a conversation in *All Over:*

> THE WIFE: *How old were you when you became aware of death?*
>
> THE BEST FRIEND: *Well... what it meant, you mean. The age we all become philosophers—fifteen?*
>
> THE WIFE: *No, no, when you were aware of it for yourself, when you knew you were at the top of the roller-coaster ride, when you knew half of it was probably over and you were on your way to it.*

To become aware that dying is a process which involves one's self is to gain self-knowledge. The process is that of moving from a state of ignorance to a state of awareness. In confronting us with the powerful presence of death, Edward Albee's plays vividly dramatize that action of becoming.

[10]Cited in William Barrett, *Irrational Man* (Garden City: Doubleday and Company), p. 145.

[11]*The New York Times*, April 18, 1971.

§ EIGHT §

THE ACT OF WAITING:
The Great Pendulum at the Still Point

VLADIMIR: *He said that Godot was sure to come tomorrow. What do you say to that?*
ESTRAGON: *Then all we have to do is to wait on here.*

The issue of what constitutes dramatic action has become much more than an academic question in the last decade or two. Ever since Aristotle wrote that tragedy shows men in action, the assumption has frequently been that dramatic action implies primarily or exclusively external deeds and incidents. But in the contemporary theatre, both here and abroad, the most dominant image is that which is usually assumed to be neither dramatic nor active, namely, waiting.

But waiting is an act; it is a decision and a choice which a man may or may not make, for even if someone says, "What else is there to do but wait?" he can reply, "Commit suicide." In despair and impatience, such a man chooses not to wait. And the act of waiting is dramatic. The complex and many-sided motivations of waiting, its inherent tension, and its attempt to discover equilibrium—all of this indicates that the act of waiting is always a becoming, a state of during. A man waiting is the human act most analogical to the suspending of a pendulum, for to be in a state of pending is to be in a time while, a space between. In that time and in that space, men and women on our theatrical stages are waiting.

— I —

Already in the theatre of the 1940s, the entire focus of *The Glass Menagerie* is to await the arrival of the Gentleman

120

Caller. In other plays of that decade, Lola is expecting Little Sheba, Blanche Dubois is awaiting Shep Huntleigh, the three inmates of Sartre's hell have abandoned all hope, for above their door is the sign No Exit, and Willy Loman is desperately hoping for a chance to escape his position of low man on the totem pole of success. The protagonists are motivated by wishes and dreams. Earlier, the Cabots of O'Neill's play had experienced desire under the elms, and Blanche Dubois wanted to ride a streetcar by that same name. Desire, as these plays portray it, is a combination of need, lust, want, and wish all held together by an anguished hope in which the past is lost and the future is bleakly oppressive. Desire is both the motivation and the goal of the waiting.

All of these plays are generally presented within the Ibsen tradition of realism. O'Neill, Arthur Miller, Tennessee Williams, and the others alluded to above listened well to Ibsen: "The illusion I wished to reproduce was that of reality. I wished to leave on the reader's mind the impression that what he had read had actually happened."[1]

In contrast, the drama of the Theatre of the Absurd has often deliberately distorted the metaphor of waiting by either impeding the action as if one were watching a slow motion film or by accelerating the frantic and frenzied activity which men do to fill in the void.

Beckett's characters, for example, seem to be virtually immobile. As Estragon says in *Waiting for Godot*: "Nothing happens, nobody comes, nobody goes, it's awful!" All objects are useless; even the suicide rope breaks. Hamm and Clov are simply waiting for the end by playing the last game, the End-game. The tramps and the clowns on their journey to the zone of zero only fidget in the void. They appear to do nothing but wait.

If existence almost comes to a halt in Beckett, it is absurdly speeded up in the work of Eugéne Ionesco. When the clock strikes seventeen in the first scene of his first play, *The Bald Soprano*, it sounds the omen for all his plays: "The universe is out of control." Ionesco has captured the ludicrous

[1]Letter to Edmund Gosse, cited in Raymond Williams, *Drama from Ibsen to Eliot* (London: Chatto and Windus, 1954), p. 61.

panic that invades us, and as he himself says, "Everything (is) raised to paroxysm . . . a theatre of violence: violently comic, violently dramatic."[2] The Old Man and the Old Woman of *The Chairs* perform a grotesque surrealistic ballet of filling the stage with dozens of chairs while waiting for the Orator. The body of the corpse in *Amédée* expands in exaggerated proportions and the couple watch the geometrical progression in horror. *The New Tenant* finds out that by frantically surrounding himself with all his possessions, he has himself become part of that which moth and rust do corrupt. If the world is being filled with a proliferation of objects, what is there to do but to bustle and hustle in furious futility? There is no time to wait.

Both of these strands, the drama of seeming inaction and the drama of maniac activity, appear to have their roots, not in the well-made plays of Ibsen or Strindberg, but in the drama of those two symbolic playwrights of the turn of the century, Chekhov and Pirandello.

A group of people are waiting for the inevitable to happen: the sale of the cherry orchard—and that waiting is the entire plot of Chekhov's play. And to fill the painful void, they have a party on the day of the sale. Madame Ranevsky comments: "It's the wrong time to have the orchestra and the wrong time to give a dance. Well, never mind." During the entire drama, the members of the family console themselves in vain hopes for a better future. They, like Firs in the poignant closing moments of the play, are waiting for the end. In another Chekhov play, three sisters are longing to go to Moscow, and nothing prevents them, as someone has said, from buying tickets on the next train—nothing except their helplessness and their half-awareness that such an action would also be futile. Within all their possibilities of promise and hope, Chekhov's people possess an impotence which prevents them from taking decisive action. In their passivity of waiting, they experience suffering in one of its most anguished forms, that of pathos.

[2]Eugène Ionesco, *Notes and Counter Notes*, trans. Donald Watson (New York: Grove Press, 1964), p. 26.

In Pirandello's masterpiece, six characters with self-conscious, passionate suffering are waiting for an author. The characters wish to be freed, and for that, they need an author. Each of them dreads waiting for the scene of the traumatic encounter of the Father and the Daughter, but each is also aware that hesitation and mere verbalizing will only prolong the agony. Thus, they make the theatre the stage of life and become aware that if all of us are merely players, then we are condemned to act out our roles without end.

In *Six Characters in Search of an Author*, as well as in many other recent plays, the cyclic rather than the linear sequence of events is enacted. Mr. and Mrs. Smith are back again in the living room at the end of *The Bald Soprano*, the teacher of *The Lesson* is ready for his forty-first victim, Genet's *Blacks* begins and ends with identical scenes, and Acts I and II of *Waiting for Godot* end with the same non-movement of Gogo and Didi. Unable to conceive of a destination, the actions of these plays coil endlessly. There is no Aristotelian beginning, middle, and end—only all middle. The not-knowing and the not-doing is the substance of the play; indeed, the action *is* the waiting.

And what is being waited for in all of these plays is a redeemer, one who will save and free those waiting from the bondage of their suffering. The exact nature of the redeemer varies: a lover who will come on a white horse to rescue the maiden in distress in Tennessee Williams' play, an author or an orator who will express the inner feelings of a family or of an old couple, or, in Clifford Odets' important play of the 1930s, all are waiting for Lefty, who is an offstage symbol of all that a man hopes for to release him from his chains of distress. All of those waiting want something or someone; they possess desires sometimes hidden to themselves and even sometimes to the audience. They hope to discover a meaning in their lives, and they are waiting for it.

The possible objects of the waiting cover a spectrum from hope to dread. The hoped-for answer to meaning may arrive, as it does for Celia in Eliot's *The Cocktail Party* and the Canterbury women in his *Murder in the Cathedral*. In other plays, a different answer than the one expected may appear:

Blanche finds herself, instead of being embraced by her ideal love Shep Huntleigh, in the arms of her brother-in-law and later being led away by a Doctor and a Matron. Instead of a savior proclaiming a message to the Old Man and the Old Woman in *The Chairs*, an orator, deaf and dumb, enters.

In several plays the one who is to redeem, the one waited for, is the one who destroys. What was hoped to be fortune transforms itself into Fate; Destiny is metamorphosed into doom. He who was thought to be the creator of the Radiant City, a Paradise, is discovered, for example, by the end of Ionesco's play to be *The Killer*, ominously silent. Bérenger pleads in vain; he has gone through all the arguments a man can set forth to find meaning in reality. He finally loses the human will to live in the face of *Tueur sans gages*, the death force, gratuitous, and purposeless. The result is terror and dread, and then the loss of hope itself, despair.

$$— II —$$

The most haunting image of waiting, however, is not that in which a hoped-for, or an unexpected, or a dread answer emerges, but that in which the waiting continues without answer or resolution. The French writer of the turn of the century, Rémy de Gourmont, prophetically described such an image:

> Hidden in mist somewhere there is an island, and on that island there is a castle, and in that castle there is a great room lit by a little lamp. And in that room people are waiting. Waiting for what? They don't know! They're waiting for somebody to knock at their door, waiting for their lamp to go out, waiting for Fear and Death. They talk. Yes, they speak words that shatter the silence of the moment. And then they listen again, leaving their sentences unfinished, their gestures uncompleted. They are listening. They are waiting. Will she come perhaps, or won't she? Yes, she will come; she always comes. But it is late, and she will not come perhaps until the morrow. The people collected under that little lamp in that great room have, nevertheless, begun to smile; they still have

hope. Then there is a knock—a *knock,* and that is all there is: And it is Life Complete, All of Life.[3]

We as well as the characters are left suspended; the knock may bring hope or destruction or a new possibility or nothing. A later French writer, Samuel Beckett, originally titled his first play simply *En attendant,* while waiting; the first production, however, was under the title *En attendant Godot.* That phrase has been absorbed into the very fabric of the mythology, the living imagery, of our time. Indeed, as Wallace Fowlie has noted, *Waiting for Godot* has given a new phrase to our language:

> *J'attends Godot,* which means that what is going on now will continue to go on for an unidentifiable length of time . . . . *J'attends Godot* is really equivalent to saying: 'this is what it means to keep on living.'[4]

Gogo and Didi face the central anxiety of man: the direct confrontation with Time. To wait and not know how to wait is to experience Time. The experience of the play indeed shows us that there is plenty of time; too much waiting means more time than things to fill it. Whenever there is nothing "to do," they remember why they are here: to wait for Godot. As Richard Schechner suggests, "their activities are therefore keeping them from a consciousness of the *action* of the play."[5]

The action is waiting; their activities are endless games: pass the hat, put on the shoes, kiss and make up, and all of the other diversions from the world of clownery and vaudeville which make the play so theatrical. They play in order to fill the painful void of boredom. But their activities also are continuous rituals—ceremonies such as the grotesque dance around the tree, incantations, and their use of invective on one another ("that's the idea, let's abuse each other"). They

[3]Cited in John Gassner, *Form and Idea in Modern Theatre* (New York: Dryden Press, 1956), p. 101.
[4]Wallace Fowlie, *Dionysius in Paris* (New York: Meridian Books, 1960), p. 210.
[5]Richard Schechner, "There's Lots of Time in *Godot,*" *Modern Drama,* IX (December, 1966), 270.

wait playfully and they wait ritualistically. Above all, they wait religiously.

And the largest question the play raises is: Are Vladimir and Estragon part of a meaningful cosmos in which Godot is the personal redeemer, or, are they merely the playthings of an impersonal fate called Godot? In brief, is the whole play a meaningful ritual in which the two are in hope and belief waiting for salvation, or, is the play a big farcical game and a microcosm of many small and meaningless games within the drama? The play's answer is neither one nor the other or both. They do not know; we as spectators do not know; and Beckett does not know. And that uncertainty is the very essence of the play. There is no absolute empirical evidence that Godot will come. There is not only conflict of testimony in the account of the two thieves, but also the little boy as the messenger whom Godot sends makes contradictory comments about Godot to the two wayfarers. The boy's only constant is that Godot will come tomorrow. The two tramps must either *believe* or *not believe* that. The act of waiting for Godot therefore is a combination of faith and absurdity, or, to use the words of the Church Fathers: *Credere quia absurdum est.*

Thus the drama is neither an affirmative retelling of the eschatological expectancy of the arrival of God, nor is it however, as many commentators have insisted, a negative portrayal of the meaningless monotony of dreary existence. The artistry of the play lies precisely in the way Beckett has perfectly balanced the hope with the hopelessness, the biblical allusions with his ironic use of them, the tragedy with the comedy. The drama, just as in *Hamlet,* is neither in the "to be" nor in the "not to be," but in the "or" which links them together.

Beckett's characters are obviously not in *Paradise,* but neither are they inhabitants, as the characters in *No Exit* and several other modern plays, of the *Inferno.* They are in *Purgatorio,* for what is central to the play is the perfect balance between salvation and damnation. Again, Beckett has given us direction both in an interview and within the play itself:

> There is a wonderful sentence in Augustine. And I wish I could remember the Latin. It is even finer in Latin than in

English. 'Do not despair: one of the thieves was saved. Do not presume: one of the thieves was damned.'[6]

The motif of the two thieves on the cross, the theme of the uncertainty of the hope of salvation and the fortuitousness of grace, permeates the whole play. Vladimir states toward the play's beginning: "One of the thieves was saved. . . . It's a reasonable percentage." Later he enlarges on the subject:

> *Two thieves. One is supposed to have been saved and the other . . . damned. . . . And yet . . . how is it that of the four Evangelists only one speaks of a thief being saved? The four of them were there—or thereabouts—and only one speaks of a thief being saved. . . . Of the other three two don't mention any thieves at all and the third says that both of them abused him.*

Since only one of the four witnesses reports it, the odds of the fifty-fifty chance have been considerably reduced. But, as Vladimir points out, it is a curious fact that everybody seems to believe that one witness: "It is the only version they know." Estragon, whose attitude has often been one of skepticism, merely comments: "People are bloody ignorant apes." But like all the other bloody ignorant apes, when the ultimate decision between hope and hopelessness is to be faced, a man will select the choice which seems to have the most hope for him, even if that choice be, as it is contemplated also by Gogo and Didi, that of suicide. For there is hope even in the realization there is nothing.

But Vladimir and Estragon do not arrive at such knowledge; they do not know there is something; they do not know there is nothing. They, like the author and many modern men, simply do not know. The drama is found in the ironic echoes of the oft-repeated line: "Nothing is certain." And, in another example, a conversation early in the play rings with both the mundane physical action of emptying one's bladder and at the same time, the metaphysical overtones of profound eschatological belief and promise:

> ESTRAGON: *What do you expect, you always wait till the last moment.*

---

[6]Cited in Harold Hobson, "Samuel Beckett, Dramatist of the Year," *International Theatre Annual*, No. 1 (London: John Calder, 1956).

VLADIMIR: (musingly). *The last moment . . . Hope deferred maketh the something sick, who said that?*
ESTRAGON: *Why don't you help me?*
VLADIMIR: *Sometimes I feel it coming all the same. Then I go all queer.*

The "it" is at one and the same time, the urge to urinate, Godot, hope, death, and all of the other desires of the human. For the reference in the passage to "hope deferred" (and that is exactly what the play dramatizes: not hope fulfilled or hope destroyed) is from Proverbs 13:12: "Hope deferred makes the heart sick, but a desire fulfilled is a tree of life." And here one of the only bits of scenery on stage takes on significance: the barren tree of life has been associated with both the damnation of man, his fall in Paradise, and with salvation, the cross of redemption. Explicitly, Gogo and Didi were told to wait by the tree. Twice, the two contemplate using the tree as a place to hang themselves. But through ineptness, fear, and most of all, the uncertainty of whether such an act will be salvatory or condemnatory, they do not carry out their plans.

Thus the powerful image of two tramps remaining in a waiting position at the end of each act is motivated neither by impotence and futility nor by a dogged religious affirmation of waiting on the mountaintops for the appearance of the Redeemer. Rather, the haunting image is one of contemporary man, who is at one and the same time, oscillating between the negation of suicide and the affirmation of commitment. Instead he chooses to wait. Existence appears tragic because the waiting may indicate there is no way out. But the situation is also comic because man preserves his imperturbability in spite of this dilemma. Neither tragic catastrophe nor comic cure is offered as an alternative by which man can triumph over his situation. The waiting itself becomes the only good.

— III —

With the mushroom cloud hovering above us, our stage is admittedly apocalyptic and despairing. The archetypal figure for the drama of despair such as Sartre's *No Exit* and Genet's

The Balcony is Sisyphus, he who is condemned to try forever to roll a rock uphill which forever is rolling back upon him. The effort is without hope; the result is despair. "We are to think clearly," Camus said, "and not hope anymore."[7]

If the image of Sisyphus is one version of man's hopelessness, another figure to convey man's frustrated aspirations is Prometheus, he who possesses *hubris*, he who presumes to be God.

Joseph Pieper in his study of hope, *Über die Hoffnung*, [8] has indicated that hopelessness can actually assume two forms: presumption or despair. Presumption is the premature, self-willed anticipation of the fulfillment of what we hope for. Despair is the premature, arbitrary anticipation of the non-fulfillment of what we hope for. Both forms of hopelessness, whether the image of Prometheus or of Sisyphus, rebel against the patience in which hope trusts. They demand impatiently either fulfillment "now already" or "absolutely no" hope. Neither is willing to wait.

It is appropriate that both of these archetypal figures find their origin in Greek mythology, for much of Greek thought considered hope an evil, an illusion because Fate is unchangeable. To Aristotle, hope was "a waking dream," to Aeschylus, "the food of exiles," and to Euripides, "man's curse." In Jean Anouilh's version of *Antigone,* the protagonist, in referring to herself, describes what hope is:

> We are of the tribe that asks questions, and we ask them to the bitter end—until no tiniest chance of hope remains to be strangled by your hands. We are of the tribe that hates your filthy hope, your docile female hope; hope your whore. . . . [9]

Indeed, at best, hope was the mixed blessing and evil which escaped last out of Pandora's box.

By contrast, the Judeo-Christian tradition finds its very meaning in the metaphor of hope. God is "the God of hope"

---

[7]Albert Camus, *The Myth of Sisyphus*, trans. Justin O'Brien (New York: Vintage Books, 1959), p. 68.

[8]Joseph Pieper, *Über die Hoffnung* (München, 1949).

[9]Jean Anouilh, *Antigone*, trans. Lewis Galantière (New York: Random House, 1946), p. 67.

(Rom. 15:13), the God with "future as his essential nature," as a recent theologian suggests, and, as Jürgen Moltmann writes, the God

> as made known in Exodus and Israelite prophecy, the God whom we therefore cannot really have in us or over us but always before us, who encounters us in his promises for the future, and whom we therefore cannot 'have' either, but can only await in active hope.[10]

For waiting is the action of the biblical drama. The people of God waited to leave Egypt and to enter the promised land of Canaan. When they were exiles in the land of Babylon, "prisoners of hope" (Zech. 9:12), God instructed Habakkuk:

> For still the vision awaits its time;
>   it hastens to the end—it will not lie.
> If it seem slow, wait for it;
>   it will surely come, it will not delay. (Hab. 2:3)

And most of all, permeating the entire history of the Old Testament, is the expectation of "the hope of Israel" (Jer. 14:8) which stretches from Jacob ("I wait for thy salvation, O Lord" Gen. 49:18) to Isaiah:

> It will be said on that day, 'Lo, this is my God; we have waited for him, that he might save us. This is the Lord; we have waited for him; let us be glad and rejoice in his salvation.' (Isa. 25:9)

The people of the New Testament, with Simeon, who was "waiting for the consolation of Israel" (Lk. 2:25), find their fulfillment in Christ Jesus, "our hope" (I Tim. 1:1). And the drama of hope still is in progress as the Jewish people await the Messiah, and as Christians "wait for the revealing of the Lord Jesus Christ" (I Cor. 1:7) and "wait for his Son from Heaven" (I Thess. 1:10).

But not only is the concept of hope tied up inextricably with the first and second coming of Jesus Christ, but also

---

[10]Jürgen Moltmann, *Theology of Hope*, trans. James W. Leitch (London: SCM Press, 1967), p. 16.

central to man's experience are the responses of despair, presumption, and hope. Job in his misery considers time a curse: "My days are swifter than a weaver's shuttle, and come to their end without hope" (Job 7:6). The Psalmist exhorts men to wait patiently for the Lord: "Be still before the Lord, and wait patiently for him . . ." (Ps. 37:7, cf. Ps. 27:14). But the prayer does not seem answered. Desperately, "out of the depths," the man of hope and hopelessness "waits for the Lord more than the watchman for the morning" (Ps. 130:1, 5). And the absence of hope reaches its deepest expression in Psalm 69:

> Save me, O God!
> For the waters have come up to my neck.
> I sink in deep mire,
>   where there is no foothold;
> I have come into deep water,
>   and the flood sweeps over me.
> I am weary with my crying;
>   my throat is parched.
> My eyes grow dim
>   with waiting for my God. (Ps. 69:1–3)

To wait is to make that complex stance of fear and expectancy, that ambigious posture of not having and of having at the same time: "Now hope that is seen is not hope. For who hopes for what he sees? But if we hope for what we do not see, we wait for it with patience" (Rom. 8:24–25). The condition of man's relation to God, as Paul Tillich points out, is "first of all one of *not* having, *not* seeing, *not* knowing, *not* grasping."[11] Since God is infinite, he is God just insofar as man does not possess Him. Man must wait for God to make Himself known. This condition of not having is certainly one of the major motifs in contemporary literature and led to that bold proclamation that God is indeed dead for a large number of people. The terror of that absence is what frequently makes the contemporary stage a modern Inferno with No Exit signs placed above all the doors.

[11]Paul Tillich, *The Shaking of the Foundations* (New York: Charles Scribner's Sons, 1948), p. 149.

Such literature places itself on the Hill of Golgotha amid the darkness and the chaos. Sisyphus and Golgotha may not be that far apart. Such a posture certainly possesses the honesty which cheap joy and cheery hope do not have. Prometheus with power hurling the rocks, and the bursting of the tomb may also not be that far apart.

But Beckett's tramps see themselves, and in them, perhaps, some of us see ourselves as lost, doubting, and wavering between despair, rebellion, and hope on that day between the two cosmic events of the Cross and the Tomb, the long Saturday.[12] Vladimir and Estragon, as usual, are uncertain about the time, but they do hover about Saturday:

> ESTRAGON: *You're sure it was this evening?*
> VLADIMIR: *What?*
> ESTRAGON: *That we were to wait.*
> VLADIMIR: *He said Saturday.* (Pause.) *I think.*
> ESTRAGON: *You think.*
> VLADIMIR: *I must have made a note of it.* (He fumbles in his pockets, bursting with miscellaneous rubbish.)
> ESTRAGON: (very insidious). *But what Saturday? And is it Saturday? Is it not rather Sunday?* (Pause.) *Or Monday?* (Pause.) *Or Friday?*
> VLADIMIR: (looking wildly about him, as though the date was inscribed in the landscape.) *It's not possible!*

Perhaps Beckett is suggesting that contemporary man's existence can best be described as the Saturday after the hope of the world seemed lost. For no day has greater potential of dramatizing the tension between faith and absurdity, of making real the action of waiting. Neither despair nor presumption is called for: it is the time between, the time of waiting. "Yes, in this immense confusion," as Vladimir says, "one thing alone is clear. We are waiting for Godot to come—" And note: this assertive statement ends with an incomplete dash.

---

[12]I am indebted to William R. Mueller and Josephine Jacobson who have suggested this idea in their essay, "Samuel Beckett's Long Saturday: To Wait or not to Wait?" in *Man in the Modern Theatre*, ed. Nathan A. Scott, Jr. (Richmond: John Knox Press, 1965), pp. 76–97.

— IV —

Lucky and Pozzo have come and gone. The Boy has brought his message: "Mr. Godot told me to tell you that he won't come this evening but surely tomorrow." Night falls. The act ends:

> Silence.
> ESTRAGON: *Well, shall we go?*
> VLADIMIR: *Yes, let's go.*
> They do not move.

Beckett closes the second act with the same words, but reverses the line assignments. The image is powerful: Godot does not yet come, the two do not go, for when presented with the choice to wait or not to wait, they opt to wait.

The words indicate the tramps' intention to stop waiting, but their action confirms their choice to wait. Futility and passiveness certainly are present, but this is balanced and kept in tension with fidelity and the active decision not to go. Their waiting confronts hopelessness, acknowledges it, grants it its rights and proper domain, but does not yield to its assault. Their action of waiting is a juggling act; it juggles faith and doubt, hope and despair. Their act of juggling consists in remaining on the side with faith and hope, and to keep doubt and despair at bay not with reason but with waiting. Waiting enlarges one's perspective beyond a present moment, without quite seeing the reason for doing so. Fortitude and endurance are beyond the merely rational. Salvation is hope, rather *hoping*, for hope is always a hoping, not a state, but a continuous action.

Martin Heidegger's discussion of *Gelassenheit,* literally "letting be," may be helpful in discerning the intricacies of the crucial act of waiting. [13] He first characterizes *Gelassenheit* as a

---

[13]Martin Heidegger, *Discourse on Thinking: A Translation of Gelassenheit,* trans. J. M. Anderson and E. H. Freund (New York: Harper and Row, 1966). Several writers have called my attention to Heidegger's ideas about waiting and its analogies to modern literature, most notably the brief fecund comments of John Killinger, *The Fragile Presence: Transcendence in Modern Literature* (Philadelphia: Fortress Press, 1973), pp. 6–7, and the

kind of "nay-saying to willing," a non-willing, or "giving up of willing." "I will not to will," Heidegger remarks, and at the same time, he insists that *Gelassenheit* is not a state of passive resignation. On the contrary, it is a "higher kind of action that is, however, no activity." It is perhaps best described as "nothing but waiting."

But waiting for what? This, according to Heidegger, cannot be specified, for as soon as we re-present and imagine—form an image of—what we are waiting for, we sink back into the subject-object relationship which reduces everything to a thing, to an object which is circumscribed by the subject's limitations. And it is precisely this subjective-objective approach that is to be transcended in *Gelassenheit*. The best one can do, therefore, is to "leave open what we are waiting for." In this manner, "the waiting lets itself in on what is Open" without attempting to bring about, and thereby violating, its openness. The region we enter in waiting is open of Itself; it is a "Region through whose magic all that belongs to It returns to where it rests." This is to say that we do not approach it at all; rather, It approaches us when we wait.

Such a posture indicates, as Killinger comments, that one is "willing to wait, interminably if need be, for what *appears*"; it cultivates, he adds, a kind of "creature patience."[14] As Eliot in "Ash Wednesday" twice enjoins us, "Teach us to sit still."

Throughout these essays, the Great Pendulum of Becoming has been swinging in free, often erratic, movement. To avoid the mechanical, the motion tends toward the animalic. Nightmare, the demonic, and the impotent threaten us, and in response, we desperately attempt to recover the connection and engage in anguished pipe dreams. For, if the mad clock which strikes seventeen at the opening of Ionesco's *The Bald Soprano* is the image which loosely unifies these capricious

---

more extended discussion of Nathan Scott in his essay, "The Literary Imagination in a Time of Dearth," in *Negative Capability: Studies in the New Literature and the Religious Situation* (New Haven: Yale University Press, 1970), pp. 59–88.

[14]Killinger, *The Fragile Presence*, pp. 6–7.

movements, then the almost static quality of Beckett's theatre provides the opposing counterpoint. "Time has stopped," Vladimir comments, and all of time, not only Pozzo's watch, has indeed seemed to come to a halt in Beckett's world. But, as usual, the next speech calls the previous assertion into question, for Pozzo responds: "Don't you believe it, Sir, don't you believe it. Whatever you like, but not that." Beckett's basic formal device is a hesitating and precarious balance which wants to avoid the temptation of nihilism, to be certain there is nothing. For when Beckett was asked what was the key word in his plays, and one can imagine how his questioner and all of his commentators were awaiting and yet dreading an answer, Beckett replied, "Perhaps."[15]

"Perhaps" is the verbal counterpart to drama's portrayal of a man waiting and to the overarching model of a great pendulum, neither in arbitrary motion nor in rigid fixity, but in suspended animation, at rest, at the still point. Eliot's image of the wheel in *Murder in the Cathedral*, which is both part of an eternal action and of an eternal patience, suggests precisely this suspendedness: "that the wheel may turn and still/ Be forever still." To stop completely is to lose the human; to be in continuous restless motion is to dwell in the regions of the inhuman and non-human, a world of entropy, a vision of the world as *machine infernale*.

"The function of art," wrote Eliot in his introduction to *The Cocktail Party*, is analogical to Dante's journey to the still point, for it is "to bring us to a condition of serenity, stillness, and reconciliation; and then leave us, as Virgil left Dante, to proceed toward a region where that guide can avail us no longer."

For the pendulum to be at the still point is for it not only to be without motion, but also in the position of "yet." Perhaps the settings of darkness on our modern stages may still turn to light, and the macabre and restless motions of their occupants may yet be transformed into stillness, and even into dancing.

[15]Cited in Tom F. Driver, "Beckett by the Madeleine," *Columbia University Forum*, IV (Summer, 1961), 20.